ANDREW DIOSY

THERE MUST BE A WAY

To the late and great Hungarian bridge writers,
Robert Darvas, Paul Lukacs, and Geza Ottlik,
whose work inspired many of the hands
appearing in this book.

MASTER POINT PRESS

Master Point Press
74 Ridelle Avenue
Toronto, Ontario
M6B 1J3
(416) 785-3924

Distributed by
Copp Clark Longman Ltd.
2775 Matheson Blvd. East
Mississauga, ON
L4W 4P7

(905) 238-6074

Canadian Cataloguing in Publication Data

Diosy, Andrew, 1924-
There must be a way: 52 bridge hands to challenge your play and defence

ISBN 0-9698461-1-8

1. Contract bridge. I. Title

GV1282.3.D56 1995	795.41'53	C95-930850-4

Cover and book design	Olena Serbyn
Editor	Linda Lee
Additional analysis	Bill Milgram

Printed and bound in Canada

1 2 3 4 5 6 7   00 99 98 97 96 95

Foreword by EDDIE KANTAR

(World Champion, WBF and ACBL Grand Master)

Do you like challenging bridge problems, some with a history? If you do, this book should be right up your alley. But first a warning: in the Introduction, it says that this book is for average club players and up; I would amend that to "above average club players", and make that "up", "way up".

Each hand highlights a beautiful offensive or defensive play. Many are such fierce battles between declarer and defender that it is almost like watching a mystery evolve. Who will triumph? Who will make the final brilliancy? The answer is "you" — but you've got to "see" it.

Personally, I find it hard to believe that anyone interested in improving their game (at the same time picking up the finer points) won't enjoy this book. I did, in spades. Even though many of the hands have appeared in print elsewhere, only someone who has read a great deal of the advanced literature will have an edge. In any case, the author has such a clever way of turning the hand around with those *&%$# questions that follow each problem that you will still be challenged even if, by chance, you happen to recognize the hand.

The format of the book also differentiates it from most other quiz books. In this book, you are shown all four hands, and then more or less told how the play went or might go. It all seems rather normal until you realize from the questions that follow that either the declarer or one or both of the defenders could have done something better. Now it is up to you to figure out what that "something" is. Always keep in mind "there must be a way".

In order to see what the author is driving at, you must have a certain degree of expertise. However, even if you don't but have a great love for the game, you will revel in the plays, mostly logical, that could have been made. Obviously, looking at all four hands allows you to make some plays that dreams are made of; it is exactly for this reason that I see "imagination development", a necessary quality for any aspiring player, as one of the big pluses of this work.

"There Must be a Way" should give you many hours of pleasure along with the inevitable occasional headache. However, any book worth its salt has a mixture of pleasure and pain, and I predict the pleasure will greatly outweigh the suffering. Therefore, my advice is to treat yourself to a gem of a book, as long as you don't try to digest it in one or two sittings. There aren't enough aspirins in the world for that!

Introduction

This is a book of "post-mortem" bridge problems for average club players and up. Unlike most "double-dummy" problems where the position of all the cards is known, these hands do not usually call for esoteric and outlandish plays or defences; indeed, many of them actually occurred at the table. But they will test your ingenuity and your powers of analysis.

Approach each hand as though you had just played it. You know the contract, and the opening lead. Now.... do you want to play or defend? What is the optimum result, given best play and defence? Can the contract be made, or is there a fiendish stratagem that will defeat it?

Many of these hands present multi-level difficulties, where each twist and turn by declarer can be countered by the ingenuity of the defence, until one or the other runs out of resources. Which side will succeed? The final solution (and in some cases, even the problem itself) will not be obvious at first glance. We have therefore presented the hands in groups of four, with the first part of the solution for each appearing on the following page. When you have reached your analytical conclusion, turn the page and read this partial solution: you may find there is a path you have yet to follow. The page after that contains the complete analysis.

Since we do not tell you at first whether a given hand *can* be made on best play and defence, you will find yourself inevitably revisiting these problems. Surely, *there must be a way*.......

NOT TOO HARD

HAND 1 • *Bravo, Professore!*

NORTH
♠ Q64
♡ 94
♢ AQJ96
♣ AQ9

WEST
♠ KJ1052
♡ 2
♢ 1042
♣ 10654

```
    N
W       E
    S
```

EAST
♠ A9873
♡ AK6
♢ K5
♣ KJ2

SOUTH
♠ ----
♡ QJ108753
♢ 873
♣ 873

Contract: 4♡
Opening Lead: ♠J

HAND 2 • *Quiet Please*

NORTH
♠ AQ7
♡ 532
♢ 6532
♣ 853

WEST
♠ J104
♡ J97
♢ 84
♣ AK962

```
    N
W       E
    S
```

EAST
♠ K983
♡ K108
♢ 10
♣ QJ1074

SOUTH
♠ 652
♡ AQ64
♢ AKQJ97
♣ ----

Contract: 5♢
Opening Lead: ♣K

HAND 3 • *Fair Exchange*

NORTH
♠ 10 9
♡ A 5 3
♢ K Q J 10 3
♣ J 8 3

WEST
♠ K Q 6 2
♡ 7
♢ 9 7 6 4
♣ 10 5 4 2

EAST
♠ A J 7 5 3
♡ K 8 2
♢ 8
♣ K 9 7 6

SOUTH
♠ 8 4
♡ Q J 10 9 6 4
♢ A 5 2
♣ A Q

Contract: 4♡
Opening Lead: ♠K

HAND 4 • *A Textbook Case*

NORTH
♠ 4
♡ K Q J 9 8 7
♢ A J 3
♣ 7 6 5

WEST
♠ K 2
♡ A 6 3
♢ Q 6 5 2
♣ 10 9 8 4

EAST
♠ Q J 10 9 8
♡ 10 5 2
♢ K 9 8
♣ Q 3

SOUTH
♠ A 7 6 5 3
♡ 4
♢ 10 7 4
♣ A K J 2

Contract: 3NT
Opening Lead: ♠K

HAND 1 • *Bravo, Professore!*

Answer Part 1

There is a story you may have read in Robert Darvas's wonderful book, *Right Through the Pack*, about the professor of logic who plays the one and only bridge hand in his life, and then gives up the game, because he finds it too easy! On that hand the professor makes a wildly illogical lead, which, of course, turns out to be the only correct one. If you have read that story, do not worry -- this is a different hand!

In our hand the opening lead of the ♠J is covered by the queen and ace, forcing declarer to ruff. South plays on trumps and East continues spade plays each time he is in with the ace and king of hearts. After drawing the last trump, South can concede a diamond trick to East and still have one more trump to ruff East's final spade return. South never plays on clubs since he can take nine tricks in the red suits (five hearts and four diamonds) plus one club.

Can this hand always be made or did East-West miss the "killing" defence?

HAND 2 • *Quiet Please*

Answer Part 1

On this hand South has four potential losers, two spades and two hearts (South can always ruff his fourth heart, if necessary). With the ♡K onside South can hold his heart losers to one by using the ♠A as an entry to reach dummy for the heart finesse. Unfortunately, the ♠K is offside so there is no help there, but with hearts 3-3 and the friendly club lead declarer could discard a spade on the fourth heart.

There are, however, some problems with this line. You ruff the opening club lead and draw trumps. You try the spade finesse first, planning to take the heart finesse later when you are in dummy. East wins and continues a spade, won in dummy by the ace. You now take the heart finesse and follow with ace and another heart, but East wins the king and his spade return defeats the contract.

Is there a better line of play?

HAND 3 • *Fair Exchange*

Answer Part 1

After winning the first trick with the ♠K, what should West continue at trick two? If he is really good, lucky, or clairvoyant he will switch to a diamond, finding his partner's singleton. However, he should never have to be so smart: East should overtake the ♠K with the ace and return a diamond, planning to get in on the trump king and return a spade to partner's queen for a diamond ruff. It doesn't even help South to play ace and another heart since East has three trumps.

Can you see a counter for this devious plot?

HAND 4 • *A Textbook Case*

Answer Part 1

This hand looks easy. South ducks the opening spade lead, and, assuming West continues spades, South wins and forces out the ♡A. West has no more spades, so South makes his contract. In fact, South will make the contract on all spade splits except when the hand that gets the lead with the ♡A has all three remaining spades. In all other cases the defence can cash at most two more spade tricks. South has nine tricks: five hearts, two clubs, one diamond, and one spade.

So, if there is a way to defeat this hand it will involve a switch at trick two. Can any switch help the defence? If so, was it correct for South to duck the first trick?

Can this hand be made?

HAND 1 • *Bravo, Professore!*

Answer Part 2

That is not the way that the professor of logic would have defended this hand; this contract *cannot* be made if you find the right return earlier. This hand is a race between declarer and the defence. Declarer must draw trumps and establish diamonds; the defence must set up a club trick before the diamonds are established.

East must switch to a club right into dummy's ace-queen; any club will do -- the king, the jack or the deuce! This has to be done when East is in with the first trump trick. Getting in with the second trump, East continues clubs, knocking out declarer's second club stopper. East will finally get to cash a club winner after winning the ◇K, defeating the contract -- the defence takes two hearts, a diamond, and a club.

Bravo, Professore!

HAND 2 • *Quiet Please*

Answer Part 2

This hand *can* be made with careful play. If you start with a spade finesse, you will need two successful finesses to make the hand; one in each major suit. You could combine your chances by improving the timing. After drawing trumps, you make the quiet lead of a small heart from hand! Suppose West wins the trick and leads a spade: declarer can afford to play the ♠Q, even though this will lose to East's king. When a spade comes back, declarer wins with dummy's ace, continues with the winning heart finesse and cashes the ♡A to draw the remaining two hearts. Now dummy's losing spade can be discarded on the established thirteenth heart. The 3-3 heart break allows you to make the hand even when one of your finesses loses.

Note that entering dummy with the ♠A and finessing the ♡Q before ducking a heart will not work. When declarer continues with the ♡A, East can throw his ♡K under it. As a result, West will get the lead on the third heart, to lead a spade through the ♠Qx remaining in dummy.

HAND 3 • *Fair Exchange*

Answer Part 2

This hand *can* be made but you have some work to do. East overtakes his partner's ♠K at trick one and returns his singleton diamond, intending to lead a spade to his partner's queen after obtaining the lead with the ♡K. But there is an effective countermeasure: at the second trick, you win East's diamond shift in dummy and lead a small club to the queen. After the successful club finesse you cash the ♣A and lead a trump to dummy's ace. No finesse this time: safely in dummy, you lead the ♣J and discard your remaining spade. This is a classic *loser-on-loser* play which prevents East from reaching his partner's hand. Now East cannot obtain a diamond ruff, so all the defence can make is a spade, a club, and the king of trumps.

HAND 4 • *A Textbook Case*

Answer Part 2

This 3NT contract *cannot* be made if you find the correct defence. West starts with the ♠K. South must duck or West will have a spade to continue with when he wins the lead with the ♡A; East will then be able to cash four spade tricks to defeat the contract. At trick two West must switch, and the only continuation which will defeat the contract is the ◇Q (this play, the sacrifice of a high card to knock out an entry, is called the Merrimac Coup). If declarer plays the ◇A, the entry to dummy's hearts is gone. If South ducks the ◇Q in dummy, the defence can continue diamonds, eventually knocking out the ace.

With the diamond entry knocked out early, South can then take only eight tricks. South has six tricks (one spade, three clubs, and two diamonds) and can get two hearts by endplaying West. To do this he must force out East's diamond entry before playing hearts. In fact, several lines are possible for *eight* tricks.

Note that if West leads a small diamond instead of the queen the defence will fail. South, in that case, can simply duck the diamond completely. East can win the ◇K but the ◇A and ◇J will remain as two entries to the dummy.

HAND 5 • A Matter of Entries

NORTH
♠ 7 3
♡ 8 6 2
◇ K J 7 4 3 2
♣ 4 2

WEST
♠ J 9 8 6 2
♡ J 9 4 3
◇ ----
♣ A 7 5 3

```
    N
W       E
    S
```

EAST
♠ 10 5 4
♡ Q 10 7 5
◇ A 10 9 8
♣ K 6

SOUTH
♠ A K Q
♡ A K
◇ Q 6 5
♣ Q J 10 9 8

Contract: 3NT
Opening Lead: ♠6

HAND 6 • Long Time No See

NORTH
♠ 10 8 5
♡ A K 3
◇ K Q J 9 6
♣ Q 3

WEST
♠ K Q J 4
♡ Q 6
◇ A 8 7 5
♣ 10 6 2

```
    N
W       E
    S
```

EAST
♠ 9 6 3
♡ 10 9 5
◇ 10 4 2
♣ K J 9 7

SOUTH
♠ A 7 2
♡ J 8 7 4 2
◇ 3
♣ A 8 5 4

Contract: 4♡
Opening Lead: ♠K

HAND 7 • *First Things First*

NORTH
♠ J 10 6 3 2
♡ Q 8
◇ A 4
♣ Q 10 9 8

WEST
♠ K 8 7
♡ 6 3
◇ J 10 9 8 5 3
♣ 7 4

EAST
♠ 9 5 4
♡ K 5 4
◇ Q 7 6
♣ A 6 5 3

SOUTH
♠ A Q
♡ A J 10 9 7 2
◇ K 2
♣ K J 2

Contract: 6♡
Opening Lead: ◇J

HAND 8 • *Inspired Play*

NORTH
♠ 7 4 3
♡ Q 10 6 3
◇ A J 2
♣ A Q J

WEST
♠ Q 9 2
♡ J 8 4 2
◇ 10 6
♣ K 9 4 3

EAST
♠ K 6
♡ A K 7
◇ 7 5 4
♣ 8 7 6 5 2

SOUTH
♠ A J 10 8 5
♡ 9 5
◇ K Q 9 8 3
♣ 10

Contract: 4♠
Opening Lead: ♡2

HAND 5 • A Matter of Entries

Answer Part 1

As declarer, you have no choice but to win the opening lead with a spade honour in hand. Counting your tricks, you have three spades and two hearts off the top; if diamonds break you can set up the diamond suit for five winners. But, as you can see, the diamonds do not break. Another alternative is to set up the club suit for three winners, but in and of itself that is not enough.

Nevertheless, forging ahead you lead a diamond to dummy's jack; East wins and leads a heart. You win and play on clubs; East wins and forces out your last heart stopper, and now when East is in on the ♣A he can cash two hearts to defeat the contract. Playing on clubs first will not help either; as long as the defence switches to hearts they will have time to establish two heart tricks, irrespective of which defender gains the lead.

Is there a better way to combine your chances in the minors?

HAND 6 • Long Time No See

Answer Part 1

Count the losers in this hand rather than the winners, using the North hand as the starting point. Assuming that hearts break 3-2 and diamonds break in a friendly manner, North has two spade losers, a potential heart loser, a diamond loser, and a club loser. Fortunately, with the trump queen coming down doubleton, there are no trump losers. If you can establish the diamonds, they will provide discards for South's clubs, allowing you to avoid a club loser.

So your plan is to give up a diamond after winning the spade lead. However, if you draw three rounds of trumps first you will not be able to get to dummy, while if you play diamonds before drawing trumps someone will ruff in and you will run out of tricks.

Can you find a solution to this problem?

HAND 7 • *First Things First*

Answer Part 1

This hand has three potential losers: a spade, a heart, and a club. However, with the ♡K onside you need not have a trump loser, and the spade loser can be discarded on dummy's fourth club. There is however a tiny problem -- entries. Suppose you win the diamond in dummy and finesse the heart: West ducks the first round and then covers the second. After drawing trumps you can lead clubs, but West waits until the third round before winning the defensive club trick and you can't get to dummy to enjoy dummy's fourth club.

Can you see an alternative plan?

HAND 8 • *Inspired Play*

Answer Part 1

West gets the defence off to its best start with a heart lead. The defence can cash one more heart trick; but is it right to do that immediately, and if so, how should the defence continue?

As declarer you count your losers: you have two heart losers and at least one trump loser, but you should have no other losers in the side suits as the diamond suit is solid. The key to the hand, then, is to hold your trump losers to one. To do this you must begin with a trump finesse. Lead a trump from dummy and put in the ten: you plan to repeat the trump finesse when you regain the lead. Conversely, the only way for the defence to defeat the hand is to take two trump tricks.

Can declarer hold his trump losers to one? What is the best defence? Who will prevail?

HAND 5 • _A Matter of Entries_

Answer Part 2

This hand _can_ be made by correct play. The seemingly natural but losing play is to lead a low diamond from hand at trick two. The problem is that you do not have the dummy entries to establish and run diamonds for four winners. Nor do you have the time to establish three diamond winners together with one or more club winners before the defence sets up major suit winners.

The winning play is to lead the ◇Q at trick two. East cannot afford to win this trick because, if he does, you can duck a diamond when you are next in, setting up four diamond winners. It will not help the defence to duck the first diamond trick, either, as in that case with one diamond trick in the bag you turn your attention to the club suit and set it up for three winners. The defence does not have time to set up and run either major suit and you wind up with nine tricks: three spades, two hearts, a diamond, and three clubs.

HAND 6 • _Long Time No See_

Answer Part 2

This hand _can_ be made with a relatively simple play, which is, nevertheless, easy to miss. You win the first or second round of spades and lead your singleton diamond: West wins, cashes his spade trick and leads a club, dummy's queen being covered by the king and the ace. You cannot draw three rounds of trumps and finish in dummy to run the diamonds. You must therefore play a trump to one of dummy's honours. At this point there are two possible continuations both of which will work.

(1) Start running diamonds, throwing clubs from your hand. East will ruff in on the fourth diamond. You overruff and re-enter dummy with the second high trump, drawing the remaining trumps from the defenders. You now cash dummy's last diamond discarding your last club.

(2) Draw only two rounds of trumps, playing the ♡4 and ♡7 from your hand; you then cash your diamond tricks. East can ruff the fourth diamond with his last trump, but you will overruff, lead the carefully preserved ♡2 to dummy's ♡3 and cash the last diamond.

Note that ducking the ◇A will not help the defenders. You simply continue diamonds while discarding a spade from your hand.

HAND 7 • *First Things First*

This hand *can* be made with careful play, but you must maximize your entries. The successful line is to win the opening lead in the closed hand and, at trick two, to lead either (1) the ♣J overtaking it with the queen in dummy or (2) the ♣2 overtaking it with the ten in dummy; in either case West has no good play. If he ducks, you finesse hearts and eventually force out the ♣A, having retained the ◇A as your dummy entry. If West wins the first round of clubs and forces out the ◇A, you can finesse in hearts and draw trumps, then re-enter dummy in the club suit to take your spade discard.

HAND 8 • *Inspired Play*

This hand *cannot* be made assuming East finds the best defensive plays at tricks two and three. East should suspect that the defence has no winners outside the trump suit, so the goal of the defence should be to set up a second trump trick. This is certainly possible if partner has Q9x of trumps. East wins the opening heart lead, cashes a second heart, and then continues with a third heart straight into dummy's tenace. Winning in dummy, declarer continues with a small trump. East plays low and the ♠J is won by West's queen. Now West makes the killing return: a fourth heart. East ruffs with the ♠K and declarer is helpless, since overruffing with the ace establishes West's ♠9 as a winner, and the contract is defeated.

HAND 9 • *Power Play*

NORTH
- ♠ 8 7 3
- ♡ K Q J 4
- ◇ J 5 2
- ♣ K 6 5

WEST
- ♠ ----
- ♡ 8 7 6 3 2
- ◇ 1 0 9 8 7
- ♣ Q 9 8 2

```
    N
  W   E
    S
```

EAST
- ♠ 9 6 4
- ♡ A 1 0 9
- ◇ Q 6 4 3
- ♣ A 1 0 7

SOUTH
- ♠ A K Q J 1 0 5 2
- ♡ 5
- ◇ A K
- ♣ J 4 3

Contract: 4♠
Opening Lead: ◇10

HAND 10 • *Endless Variety*

NORTH
- ♠ J 9
- ♡ A 9 5 3
- ◇ A J 1 0 9
- ♣ J 1 0 5

WEST
- ♠ K 7 6 4 2
- ♡ 8
- ◇ Q 5 4 3 2
- ♣ 9 7

```
    N
  W   E
    S
```

EAST
- ♠ A 5
- ♡ K 1 0 7
- ◇ 8 7 6
- ♣ 8 6 4 3 2

SOUTH
- ♠ Q 1 0 8 3
- ♡ Q J 6 4 2
- ◇ K
- ♣ A K Q

Contract: 4♡
Opening Lead: ◇2

HAND 11 • *Short Clubs*

NORTH
♠ K
♡ 9 5 4 2
♦ K 7
♣ K Q J 8 6 5

WEST
♠ 8 6
♡ K J 10 6 3
♦ A J 9 6 5
♣ 7

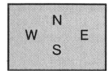

EAST
♠ 7 4
♡ A Q 8
♦ Q 4 3
♣ A 10 4 3 2

SOUTH
♠ A Q J 10 9 5 3 2
♡ 7
♦ 10 8 2
♣ 9

Contract: 4♠
Opening Lead: ♣7

HAND 12 • *Four Kings*

NORTH
♠ 7 4
♡ Q 8 3
♦ A Q J 7 6
♣ 10 3 2

WEST
♠ 8 3
♡ 7 5 2
♦ 10 8 5 2
♣ A 7 6 4

EAST
♠ A J
♡ A J 10 6 4
♦ 4
♣ Q J 9 8 5

SOUTH
♠ K Q 10 9 6 5 2
♡ K 9
♦ K 9 3
♣ K

Contract: 4♠
Opening Lead: ♡7

HAND 9 • *Power Play*

Answer Part 1

3NT would have been an easier contract, but you have arrived in 4♠. Winning the first trick with the ◇A, you count your losers: one heart loser and three potential club losers. Leading up to dummy's ♣K does not work since the ace is in the East hand. However, once you force out the ♡A, the heart winners in dummy can provide a parking spot for South's clubs. If trumps split 2-1 you can enter dummy on a third trump to cash the hearts, once the ace is forced out. Unfortunately, with the bad trump break, there is no entry to dummy; or is there?

HAND 10 • *Endless Variety*

Answer Part 1

At first, this hand appears very simple: it seems that you have two spade losers and a heart loser. So it looks easy enough to win the ◇K, draw trumps, and then give up the ♠A and ♠K to establish the remaining two spades in hand. But there is a danger: East has the ♡10 and could score a spade ruff.

One possibility is to play a heart to the ace and another heart, but then East could win the ♡K and play the ♠A and another spade; when West continues a third spade, East can overruff dummy's ♡9. Another option is to lead the ♡Q and finesse into East's king. If you try that, then when West plays the third spade through you will be able to trump high in dummy, but this will still establish a trump trick in East's hand.

Is there another plan which will work better?

HAND 11 • *Short Clubs*

Answer Part 1

This hand can take several twists and turns depending on how the defence proceeds. Suppose East wins the opening lead with the ♣A and cashes the ♡A; with the ◊A onside you have two more potential losers, both diamonds. But there are two possible ways to handle the second diamond loser: ruff it or throw it on the good clubs in dummy.

Do you have any more challenges? Is there some defence which will cause you a problem? Can this hand be made?

HAND 12 • *Four Kings*

Answer Part 1

In order to set up a diamond ruff, East wins the opening lead with the ♡A and leads back his singleton diamond. As declarer, you count your losers: you have three off the top (one spade, one heart, and one club), so you can't afford to have a diamond ruffed as well. The problem is that you can't draw trumps without giving up the lead to the ♠A; East will then return a club to his partner's ace and receive his diamond ruff. If only East had both black aces you could make this hand, because West would not have an entry to give his partner that ruff.

Is there some way to keep West off lead, or does this one belong to the defence?

HAND 9 • *Power Play*

Answer Part 2

This hand *can* be made. After winning the opening lead with the ◇A, you lead the ♠A, and see the bad break. You still, however, need a trump entry to dummy. This can be established, but first you must set up your heart winners. So at trick three you lead a heart to dummy's king and East's ace; back comes a diamond to your king.

Now you are prepared to sacrifice one trump trick to make two heart tricks, so you immediately lead a small trump to dummy's ♠7! It doesn't matter whether East ducks or wins, you will still be able to reach dummy's hearts. If he ducks, you cash two hearts right away, discarding clubs from hand. If he wins the trick and leads back a diamond, you make sure to ruff high. That allows you to save a small spade to lead to dummy's ♠8 so that you can cash the now good hearts, discarding two clubs from your hand. You lose only one club, one trump, and the ♡A.

HAND 10 • *Endless Variety*

Answer Part 2

This hand *can* be made. The danger is that East when in with the ♡K, he can play spades to establish a second trump trick for the defence. To prevent this, you must win the opening lead with the ◇A in dummy, and lead a small trump! If East goes up with the king and leads spades as before, declarer can ruff the third round with the ♡A and still have high trumps to draw the remaining two rounds and take the rest of the tricks. In order to make this hand, you must lead *away* from a top honour to achieve a strategic purpose, an example of the endless variety of bridge.

HAND 11 • *Short Clubs*

Answer Part 2

This hand ***cannot*** be made. East wins the opening club lead with the ace, cashes the ♡A, and leads a diamond which West must duck to the king. This removes the entry to dummy's club winners before trumps have been drawn. If declarer now tries to play clubs, West will ruff in. If declarer draws trumps instead, he will not be able to get back to dummy to play clubs and will lose two diamonds. Declarer's only chance at this point is to try to ruff a diamond in dummy. That is why it is so important for the defence to duck the first diamond at trick two. After the duck, if South tries to lead a second diamond, West can return a trump eliminating South's last chance. If West errs by winning the ◇A at trick three, declarer either gets to ruff a diamond in dummy, or retains his entry to the clubs, depending on whether West plays a diamond or a trump next.

HAND 12 • *Four Kings*

Answer Part 2

This hand ***can*** be made. In order to get a ruff, East wins the opening lead with the ♡A and leads his singleton diamond. Your goal as declarer is to keep the danger hand (West) off lead. To do that you must get rid of your club loser, and you are willing to trade it for another loser if necessary. To that end you must throw the ♡K under the ace to unblock the heart suit, win the diamond return, and play the ♡Q and another heart. Fortunately, East must win the third heart and you happily deposit the ♣K on this trick. This loser-on-loser play disrupts the communication between the defenders.

East can try his best to defeat the contract by returning a fourth heart but with the fortunate distribution in the spade suit your ten will win the trick. You now force out the ♠A and ruff the pesky heart return with the ♠9. The ♠K draws the last two trumps and you are home: you have lost only one spade and two heart tricks.

HAND 13 • *The Sooner the Better*

NORTH
- ♠ 8 6 5
- ♡ 9 7 3
- ◇ 6 5 4 2
- ♣ A J 9

WEST
- ♠ J 10 9 3
- ♡ Q 6 4
- ◇ Q J
- ♣ K 6 5 3

EAST
- ♠ Q 2
- ♡ J 10
- ◇ 10 8 7 3
- ♣ Q 10 8 7 2

SOUTH
- ♠ A K 7 4
- ♡ A K 8 5 2
- ◇ A K 9
- ♣ 4

Contract: 4♡
Opening Lead: ◇Q

HAND 14 • *Belladonna's Class*

NORTH
- ♠ A Q 9 3
- ♡ 8 3
- ◇ J 9
- ♣ 9 7 6 5 2

WEST
- ♠ J 8 6
- ♡ K 7
- ◇ A 5 3 2
- ♣ Q J 10 3

EAST
- ♠ K 10 5 4 2
- ♡ 4
- ◇ K 10 8 7
- ♣ K 8 4

SOUTH
- ♠ 7
- ♡ A Q J 10 9 6 5 2
- ◇ Q 6 4
- ♣ A

Contract: 4♡
Opening Lead: ♣Q

Hand 15 • *Nothing Simpler*

NORTH
♠ 8 2
♡ J 5
◇ A 8 7 5 4
♣ 9 6 4 3

WEST
♠ J 10 9
♡ 9 6 3
◇ Q 10 6 3
♣ K J 2

```
        N
   W         E
        S
```

EAST
♠ 5 3
♡ K 10 7 4
◇ K J 9 2
♣ Q 10 5

SOUTH
♠ A K Q 7 6 4
♡ A Q 8 2
◇ ----
♣ A 8 7

Contract: 4♠
Opening Lead: ♠J

HAND 16 • *All the Right Spots*

NORTH
♠ 7 6 5
♡ A K J 10 7 2
◇ 5 2
♣ A 8

WEST
♠ 8
♡ 9 6 5 4
◇ 9 7
♣ 10 7 6 5 4 2

```
        N
   W         E
        S
```

EAST
♠ A K 4
♡ Q
◇ A Q J 10 8 3
♣ J 9 3

SOUTH
♠ Q J 10 9 3 2
♡ 8 3
◇ K 6 4
♣ K Q

Contract: 4♠
Opening Lead: ◇9

HAND 13 • *The Sooner the Better*

Answer Part 1

Declarer has four potential losers in this hand. The loss of a diamond and a trump cannot be avoided, but what about spades? If the suit divided evenly there would be no problem, but with the 4-2 division there is a danger of losing two spade tricks. Obviously, to make the contract one has to ruff a losing spade in dummy. What about starting with two high trumps, followed by two top spades and a third spade? That won't work because West will win the spade, cash the ♡Q and still score the ♠J as well, while your diamond loser has not gone anywhere. The alternative is to start with three rounds of spades before drawing trumps; however, West can win the third spade and lead a fourth spade, and East will overruff the dummy.

So far the defence is in command. Can this hand be made?

HAND 14 • *Belladonna's Class*

Answer Part 1

The problem on this hand is to avoid losing three diamond tricks: there is an inevitable trump loser so the diamond losers must be held to two. After winning the first trick with the ♣A, you must defer drawing trumps so that you can ruff a diamond if necessary. You start by leading a diamond to the nine: West must duck and East will win the ◇10. East will now return a trump, and it doesn't matter whether you rise or duck, the defence will have an opportunity to remove dummy's trumps, either immediately or when West is in on the ◇A.

Is there a way to make this hand?

HAND 15 • *Nothing Simpler*

Answer Part 1

West has definitely found the best lead, a trump, which can prevent you from ruffing a losing heart in dummy. As declarer, you count your losers: two hearts and two clubs. If you could get to dummy you would be able to make ten tricks by throwing one of your losers on the ◇A, but how can you do that? When this hand was actually played, declarer led a low heart to the jack at trick two; East won the king and then returned a trump, ending any chance of a ruff and removing all chance of getting to the dummy.

Can you see a way to dummy or will the excellent defenders prevail?

HAND 16 • *All the Right Spots*

Answer Part 1

You have three losers off the top in your 4♠ contract, two spades and a diamond, and there is significant risk of some sort of ruff (West might have a singleton diamond, or a doubleton diamond and three trumps, and so on). But as you can see, none of these risks are really extant on this hand.

Is there anything the defence can do? Does declarer need a safety play of some sort? Or is this one of those cut-and-dried safe contracts?

HAND 13 • *The Sooner the Better*

Answer Part 2

This hand *can* be made; it is a matter of timing, and the solution is really quite simple. After winning the first trick in hand you lead a small spade immediately: now nothing can hurt you. On regaining the lead, you cash the two top trumps and then play the ♠A and ♠K. Now you can safely ruff the last spade on the board. All the enemy can make is a trump, a diamond, and a spade.

HAND 14 • *Belladonna's Class*

Answer Part 2

This hand *can* be made. The problem is to avoid losing three diamond tricks. The instinctive play is to lead a diamond from the closed hand toward the dummy and finesse the ◇9 when West plays low, but this does not work on this hand. The key is to make sure that West wins the first diamond trick, and to do this you cross to dummy on the ♠A and lead the ◇9 from dummy.

East cannot afford to rise on the ◇K because this will allow you to set up a diamond trick by force since you will still have the ◇J and ◇Q remaining. The best East can do is cover the ◇9 with the ◇10, but you can counter by covering the ◇10 with the ◇Q. West wins with the ◇A but he cannot play trumps without losing the defence's trump trick. Suppose West continues a club: you ruff in your hand and lead another diamond, West's king winning. When he returns a trump you go up with the ace and ruff your third diamond in dummy.

There is a story to this hand: when it occurred some years ago in a rubber bridge game, the great Italian star, Giorgio Belladonna, picked the winning line after hardly a moment's thought!

HAND 15 • *Nothing Simpler*

Answer Part 2

This hand *can* be made. There is a simple winning line, which nevertheless is difficult to perceive. After winning the opening trump lead in your hand, you should lead the ♡Q, instead of the ♡2! This simple play ensures the contract. If East takes the ♡K and continues a trump (best), you can enter dummy on the ♡J and cash the ◇A, discarding a club. You make the contract with two heart tricks, six spades, a diamond, and a club. If East ducks the ♡Q, you will make eleven tricks! You continue with the ♡A, ruff a heart, and discard a loser on the ◇A: your only losers will be a heart and a club.

HAND 16 • *All the Right Spots*

Answer Part 2

This hand *cannot* be made if the defence finds the winning line. The key play for the defence is for you, as East, to duck the opening diamond lead with any card but the ◇3! Declarer wins the ◇K and attacks trumps: now you win and shift to your singleton ♡Q. Declarer continues trumps but you are ready for that: you hop up with the trump ace and lead back your ◇3 hoping partner has the ◇7. Partner wins the ◇7 and gives you your heart ruff!

If declarer leads a diamond at trick two in the hope of destroying the defensive communications, you win the diamond and lead a third diamond: West will be able to over-ruff dummy with the ♠8. It is indeed fortunate that West has all the right spot cards.

SECTION 2

PRETTY DIFFICULT

HAND 17 • *Give Up?*

NORTH
♠ J 5
♡ 10 6 2
◇ Q 10 4
♣ A 10 8 5 3

WEST
♠ A 9 7 6 3 2
♡ 8 5 4
◇ 5
♣ 9 7 4

EAST
♠ K Q 10 8
♡ K 7 3
◇ K J 6
♣ Q J 6

SOUTH
♠ 4
♡ A Q J 9
◇ A 9 8 7 3 2
♣ K 2

Contract: 5◇
Opening Lead: ♠A

HAND 18 • *A Sort of Bath Coup*

NORTH
♠ 10 9 4
♡ 6
◇ A J 10 6
♣ A Q 10 8 5

WEST
♠ 8 3
♡ 7 5 3
◇ Q 9 8 7
♣ 7 6 4 3

EAST
♠ K Q 7 5 2
♡ A 10
◇ K 5
♣ K J 9 2

SOUTH
♠ A J 6
♡ K Q J 9 8 4 2
◇ 4 3 2
♣ ----

Contract: 4♡
Opening Lead: ♠8

HAND 19 • *Four Losers*

NORTH
♠ A 6 3
♡ J 7 6 3
◇ K 2
♣ A J 10 8

WEST
♠ 10 8
♡ K 5
◇ 10 8 6 5 4
♣ 7 6 5 3

EAST
♠ Q J 2
♡ A Q 10 9 4 2
◇ A J 9
♣ 2

SOUTH
♠ K 9 7 5 4
♡ 8
◇ Q 7 3
♣ K Q 9 4

Contract: 4♠
Opening Lead: ♡K

HAND 20 • *Favourable Cards*

NORTH
♠ A 8 3
♡ Q 8
◇ 10 9 5 4
♣ 9 7 6 2

WEST
♠ K J 7 6 2
♡ ----
◇ K J 8 3
♣ K Q 10 4

EAST
♠ 10 5
♡ J 10 9 4
◇ Q 6 2
♣ J 8 5 3

SOUTH
♠ Q 9 4
♡ A K 7 6 5 3 2
◇ A 7
♣ A

Contract: 4♡
Opening Lead: ♣K

HAND 17 • _Give Up?_

Answer Part 1

After the opening lead of the ♠A, assume that West continues spades (there is no better continuation) and South ruffs. At first it appears that declarer has only two losers: the ♠A and a trump. The problem on this hand becomes apparent when you try to work out an exact line of play: South is short of dummy entries. If South enters dummy with the ♣A and leads the ◇Q, East covers, and there is no way to re-enter dummy to take the heart finesse. South could try leading a high diamond spot from his hand now to promote the ◇10 as a dummy entry, but East could just duck and win the third diamond. And if South starts by leading the ◇10 from dummy, East covers with the jack and we arrive at a similar position -- East holds off the ◇K until declarer plays the ◇Q. As a result, declarer will lose three tricks, one each in spades, diamonds, and hearts.

So, can this hand be made?

HAND 18 • _A Sort of Bath Coup_

Answer Part 1

South reached a sound contract on this deal, leaving only one small detail remaining: making the hand. When West led the ♠8, declarer could draw the obvious conclusion that this was likely to be from a doubleton. The danger was that when East got in with the ♡A, he would cash a high spade and give his partner a ruff. But South visualized a line of play that would allow him to make 4♡: he ducked the opening spade lead, throwing the ♠J under the ♠Q! This is a sort of Bath Coup, used to disrupt the communications between the enemy hands.

Now when East continues spades, South can duck the return to the ♠10, throw away his ♠A on the ♣A, then lead a trump from the dummy. If East wins and returns a spade, South can ruff the spade high, draw trumps, and finesse the diamonds twice to make his contract. South will lose only one heart, one spade, and one diamond.

Do you see any fly in the ointment?

HAND 19 • *Four Losers*

Answer Part 1

After the lead of the ♡K, West's best line is to continue with another heart. South inevitably has a spade loser and a heart loser and so he must hold his diamond losers to one to make the hand. How should declarer proceed?

If he draws two rounds of trumps and then leads a diamond to the king, East will win and draw dummy's last trump, leaving South with a second diamond loser. If he leads a diamond to the queen (which will hold the trick) followed by a second diamond, East will win the ◇A and then cash the ♠Q and the ◇J for down one. Another option is to lead a diamond before drawing two rounds of trumps; this will fail because East, on winning the diamond, will lead a high heart promoting a second trump trick for the defence.

Is there any way to solve this conundrum?

HAND 20 • *Favourable Cards*

Answer Part 1

At first this hand looks easy: it appears that you will have a diamond loser and either one or two spade losers. However, after winning the ♣A you lead a heart to the ace and get the bad news: you also have a heart loser. You must now hold your spade losers to one; however, with the ♠K in the West hand, leading up to the queen will not work. You are missing the ♠J and ♠10, and it seems that you will inevitably lose another spade trick.

Can you see any way to produce another trick? Hint: there is no squeeze or endplay.

HAND 17 • *Give Up?*

Answer Part 2

This hand *can* be made with careful play. South can pro-mote a second entry to the dummy by leading the ◇9 from his hand at trick three, ducking the trick to East's jack. East must win or South can simply cash the ◇A and use his dummy entry to take heart finesses. East therefore wins the ◇J, and South will win the club continuation in dummy with the ♣A. Now the ◇Q is led from dummy. If East covers, South wins and can re-enter dummy with the ◇10 to take two heart finesses. If East ducks, the lead remains in dummy and South is now free to take heart finesses.

At the table this line would make sense on hands where East is marked with most of the high cards. For example, if East had opened the bidding 1NT, he would be marked with all the remaining high cards after West starts the ♣A; therefore, East must have the diamond honours and the heart finesse must work.

HAND 18 • *A Sort of Bath Coup*

Answer Part 2

This hand *cannot* be made with best defence. South had a beautiful plan and it deserved to succeed, but life isn't like that. When East held the first trick with the ♠Q, he did not continue with a small spade but led the ♠K instead. This re-turn destroys South's communication to the dummy: if South does not discard a spade on the ♣A, he will lose a di-amond, a heart, a spade, and a spade ruff whether he ducks or wins the first spade.

Therefore South must forego the double diamond fi-nesse and cross to dummy on the ◇A to throw his last spade on the ♣A. South is now in danger of losing two diamond tricks, along with a spade and a heart for down one. The di-amond suit is blocked and when East is in on the trump ace, only one diamond can be cashed. However, with all the en-tries to dummy gone there is no squeeze and West will even-tually score his second diamond trick.

HAND 19 • *Four Losers*

Answer Part 2

In spite of the four apparent losers (a trump, a heart, and two diamonds), this hand *can* be made on a dummy reversal! The winning line is to play the king and ace of trumps in that order, and lead a diamond from dummy (playing the ♠A, then the ♣K, and crossing to dummy on a club also works). East cannot win the ◇A since that would give declarer two diamond tricks, the queen and the king. Now South sets up the North hand by ruffing two more hearts in the South hand using the clubs as entries, then cashes his remaining club winners, letting East take the ♠Q whenever he wants. The play would go: ◇Q, ♣J, heart ruff, ♣A, heart ruff, then cash two clubs. East can ruff in at any time and will ultimately score the ♠Q and the ◇A. South loses only three tricks (one spade, one heart, and one diamond).

HAND 20 • *Favourable Cards*

Answer Part 2

This hand *can* be made if you correctly visualize the location of the adverse cards. While in dummy with the ♡Q you lead a small spade and put in the ♠9: you are finessing against the ♠10 or ♠J in the East hand. This play is called an *intrafinesse* - you are finessing an interior card with the goal of forcing the long hand to take one of the defence's spade winners. After you regain the lead and draw two more rounds of trumps, you now lead the ♠Q from your hand. Bingo! It does not matter whether West covers or not, as you smother East's ♠10, killing two birds with one stone. You lose only one spade trick, a trump, and a diamond.

HAND 21 • *Mrs. Guggenheim*

NORTH
- ♠ J 10 9 3
- ♡ A J 7 4
- ◇ J 3
- ♣ A Q 3

WEST
- ♠ Q 7 5
- ♡ Q 9 5
- ◇ K 4 2
- ♣ 10 9 6 5

EAST
- ♠ K 8 6 2
- ♡ K 10 6 3
- ◇ 7 5
- ♣ K 8 4

SOUTH
- ♠ A 4
- ♡ 8 2
- ◇ A Q 10 9 8 6
- ♣ J 7 2

Contract: 3NT
Opening Lead: ♣10

HAND 22 • *Drawing Trumps*

NORTH
- ♠ J 5
- ♡ A K Q 2
- ◇ A K 8 6 2
- ♣ Q J

WEST
- ♠ Q 10 9 7
- ♡ 8 6
- ◇ 4 3
- ♣ K 8 7 6 2

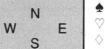

EAST
- ♠ 6
- ♡ J 9 5 4
- ◇ J 10 9 5
- ♣ 10 9 4 3

SOUTH
- ♠ A K 8 4 3 2
- ♡ 10 7 3
- ◇ Q 7
- ♣ A 5

Contract: 6♠
Opening Lead: ♡8

HAND 23 • *Overbid*

NORTH
♠ A K 10
♡ A J
♢ Q 8 6
♣ A 8 6 4 2

WEST
♠ 7 6 4
♡ Q 9 8
♢ A K J 10
♣ K J 9

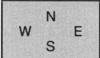

EAST
♠ ----
♡ 7 6 5 4 2
♢ 9 7 5 4 3 2
♣ 10 7

SOUTH
♠ Q J 9 8 5 3 2
♡ K 10 4
♢ ----
♣ Q 5 3

Contract: 6♠
Opening Lead: ♢K

HAND 24 • *There Must Be A Way*

NORTH
♠ 7 6 5 4 2
♡ ----
♢ A 9 8 7
♣ A J 10 9

WEST
♠ K Q J 10
♡ J 8 6 5 3
♢ K J 2
♣ 2

EAST
♠ 9 8 3
♡ K 10 9 7 4 2
♢ Q 10
♣ Q 3

SOUTH
♠ A
♡ A Q
♢ 6 5 4 3
♣ K 8 7 6 5 4

Contract: 3NT
Opening Lead: ♠K

HAND 21 • *Mrs. Guggenheim*

Answer Part 1

When this hand was played some years ago in a rubber bridge game, a small club was played from the dummy at trick one and East won the ♣K. East continued with a small spade and the contract was already doomed. South, a young man who didn't know yet that nothing ever works, at least not in bridge, relied on a successful diamond finesse (remember, he had not seen the opponents' hands).   He won the spade trick with the ace in his hand, entered dummy with a club, and led the ◊J. Things looked good for a moment when the ◊J won, but when the diamond finesse was repeated West won with the ◊K. West continued with the ♡9 and the defence finished up with three heart tricks, two spade tricks, a diamond, and a club. Down three! South's partner was convinced that there must be a better line of play, and he suggested taking the ♣A at trick one.

Was he right? Was there a better way to play the hand? Should South take the ♣A at trick one? Can this hand be made?

HAND 22 • *Drawing Trumps*

Answer Part 1

You have three potential losers on this hand: a club and two trumps. However, you can plan to throw the club loser on one of dummy's long diamonds. The key to the hand, therefore, is to hold your trump losers to one. After winning the opening lead in dummy, you cross to your hand with the ◊Q to lead a trump towards the jack -- this is a standard play designed to restrict your losers in this suit to one; West rises with the ♠Q (best). Now if West continues hearts, you have an easy road. Taking the trick in dummy, you cash the ♠J, return to your hand with the ♣A, draw trumps, and dispose of the losing club on the long diamond.

What about a different return when the defence is in with the ♠Q? Can declarer make the hand on any defence?

HAND 23 • *Overbid*

Encouraged by your fantastic play on previous hands, your rubber bridge partner overbids again and puts you into 6♠. Can you repeat past performances?   After studying the hand for a while, you realize that you have eleven tricks: three hearts (assuming you can find the ♡Q), seven spades, and a club.   It does not appear possible to set up clubs without losing two tricks. However, where there are eleven tricks, perhaps there are twelve?   Can you find a way to make this hand?   Remember, it's your money!

HAND 24 • *There Must Be A Way*

After winning the opening spade lead, it appears that, with the club suit splitting, declarer has nine tricks: one spade, one heart, one diamond, and six clubs.   There is, however, one minor problem -- the club suit is blocked and there is no entry to the South hand once the ♠A is knocked out. Various possibilities come to mind since the ♡K is onside. You could try to set up the fifth spade in dummy, but then East-West could shift to diamonds and establish three spade tricks and two diamond tricks.   No, the key to this hand must surely be in finding a way to disentangle the club suit.

Can this be done?

HAND 21 • *Mrs. Guggenheim*

Answer Part 2

This hand *can* be made, but the correct play is not the one suggested by North. If South takes the ♣A at trick one, West wins the second round of diamonds and switches to the ♡9; declarer now has eight tricks: five diamonds, a heart, a spade, and a club. Declarer ducks the ♡9. Now, if the defence continues hearts, declarer is home. (He would win the ♡Q and concede a club -- East can take only one more heart trick. Similarly if West leads a small heart, declarer wins the ace blocking the suit.) But suppose that when declarer ducks the ♡9 at trick four, East overtakes with the ♡10 and switches to a spade: this sets up five defensive tricks (two spades, a heart, a club, and a diamond).

How would Mrs. Guggenheim, the naive player in S. J. Simon's classic *Why You Lose at Bridge,* play this hand? Why, she would simply finesse the ♣Q at the first trick! Amazingly, this straightforward play ensures the contract by preserving an entry to the South hand. Taking the ♣K, East must switch to hearts, and this trick goes to the queen and ace. Diamonds are now led and West wins the ◇K. West continues with the ♡9, covered by the jack, and East wins the ♡K. At this stage, the defence can take only one more heart trick before declarer regains the lead, and then the rest of the tricks belong to South.

HAND 22 • *Drawing Trumps*

Answer Part 2

This hand *cannot* be made, which is hardly surprising in view of the fact that most of the enemy's trumps are stacked in West's hand. After winning the queen of trumps, West does not lead a heart, but leads the ♣K instead! (This play is called a Merrimac Coup). West is sacrificing the ♣K, but this is not a trick that he would have been able to score in any case. The purpose of this play is to remove an entry to declarer's hand. Now South is helpless. South must win the trick with the ace in his hand and lead a spade to dummy's jack, but he cannot return safely to his hand. He can cash the ♣J and a top diamond, but when he tries to ruff another diamond to his hand, West will overruff, setting the contract.

HAND 23 • *Overbid*

Twelve tricks *can* be made on a diamond-club squeeze. You duck the opening lead discarding a club from your hand, and eventually come down to the following position:

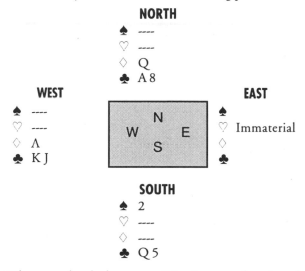

NORTH
♠ ----
♡ ----
◇ Q
♣ A 8

WEST
♠ ----
♡ ----
◇ Λ
♣ K J

EAST
♠
♡ Immaterial
◇
♣

SOUTH
♠ 2
♡ ----
◇ ----
♣ Q 5

When you play the last trump West is squeezed, and you have managed to lose only the very first trick. Your partner was justified in his confidence in you. Note that ruffing the opening lead and later ducking a club will not work since East can win the club and continue clubs, eliminating the club entry to dummy needed for the squeeze.

HAND 24 • *There Must Be A Way*

This hand *can* be made since declarer can overcome the problem of the club blockage. The solution is to lead the ♡Q from the closed hand at trick two and discard a small club from dummy East will win the ♡K and, say, return a spade, the contract is secure. On regaining the lead, South will cash two high clubs ending in hand and then throw dummy's last club on the ♡A. After that he can cash the remaining clubs and make his contract with six club tricks and the other three aces.

HAND 25 • *Now or Never*

NORTH
♠ K 75
♡ Q 5
◇ 7 6 5 4 3
♣ 7 6 2

WEST
♠ 4 3 2
♡ A 8 7 3
◇ K Q 10 9
♣ 8 5

```
        N
    W       E
        S
```

EAST
♠ J 9 8 6
♡ 6 4
◇ A J 2
♣ J 10 9 3

SOUTH
♠ A Q 10
♡ K J 10 9 2
◇ 8
♣ A K Q 4

Contract: 4♡
Opening Lead: ◇K

HAND 26 • *Marked Finesse*

NORTH
♠ K 7
♡ K 5 4 2
◇ 5 4 2
♣ 10 9 4 3

WEST
♠ J 9 6 4 3 2
♡ Q 8 7
◇ 3
♣ K 6 2

```
        N
    W       E
        S
```

EAST
♠ Q 10 8
♡ A J 9 6 3
◇ K 8
♣ J 8 5

SOUTH
♠ A 5
♡ 10
◇ A Q J 10 9 7 6
♣ A Q 7

Contract: 5◇
Opening Lead: ♠4

HAND 27 • *Trump Control*

NORTH
- ♠ K Q 3 2
- ♡ A K
- ◊ A Q 7 6
- ♣ 8 6 3

WEST
- ♠ A 10 9
- ♡ 10 9 5 4
- ◊ K J 10 8 2
- ♣ A

EAST
- ♠ J 8 7
- ♡ 2
- ◊ 9 5 4
- ♣ K 10 9 7 5 2

SOUTH
- ♠ 6 5 4
- ♡ Q J 8 7 6 3
- ◊ 3
- ♣ Q J 4

Contract: 4♡
Opening Lead: ♣A

HAND 28 • *Squeeze Possibilities*

NORTH
- ♠ K J 5
- ♡ K Q 5
- ◊ K 7 5 2
- ♣ A 9 8

WEST
- ♠ 6 4
- ♡ J 10 9 7
- ◊ Q J 10 9
- ♣ 7 3 2

EAST
- ♠ 8 3
- ♡ 8 6 4 2
- ◊ A 8 6 3
- ♣ Q J 10

SOUTH
- ♠ A Q 10 9 7 2
- ♡ A 3
- ◊ 4
- ♣ K 6 5 4

Contract: 6♠
Opening Lead: ◊Q

HAND 25 • *Now or Never*

Answer Part 1

When this hand was played some years ago in a teams championship, at one table the declarer failed to make the contract. After winning the first trick, West continued diamonds and South ruffed. Next, declarer led a trump to the queen and a trump back. West won his ace and shortened the South hand again by leading another diamond. South had to ruff and when the trumps failed to break evenly, he tried to cash his club winners. But West ruffed the third club and cashed his remaining diamond for the setting trick.

Things didn't go quite the same way at the other table. Does declarer have an alternative line that will succeed or should the defence prevail?

HAND 26 • *Marked Finesse*

Answer Part 1

As declarer in 5◊, you have four potential losers -- a heart, a diamond, and two clubs. However, with the ◊K onside, you do not have to lose a trump trick, and although the ♣K is offside you can also hold your club losers to one, since the ♣J is onside. The problem is how to get to dummy to take all these finesses. Let us say that you win the spade in dummy and take the diamond finesse. After that wins you can draw the remaining trumps, but now what? There doesn't appear to be an endplay.

Is there another line, or will the defence prevail even with this lucky layout?

HAND 27 • *Trump Control*

Answer Part 1

This hand is a good example of a hand where trump control is the key field of battle. West starts with the ♣A and switches to a trump which you must win in dummy; you then cash the second top heart. You have three top losers, two clubs and a spade, so you cannot afford to lead a club before drawing trumps since East would win and give his partner a club ruff.

So you must get back to your hand to draw the remaining trumps. Let us say that you now lead the ace and another diamond, ruffing in your hand. You can now draw the remaining trumps, leaving only one trump in your hand, and lead a spade to the dummy. West ducks, and you win with one of the spade honours in dummy. But you are now at the end of your resources. You can lead a club, but East will win and force you with a diamond. You can now cash a high club, but when you lead a spade West wins and cashes a diamond, defeating the contract.

Is there a better line or is declarer truly at the end of his rope?

HAND 28 • *Squeeze Possibilities*

Answer Part 1

With clubs 3-3 you have two losers: one diamond and one club. Unfortunately, after the diamond lead the third heart in dummy does not provide a useful discard. Clearly the only way to make this hand is with a squeeze, and it must therefore be right to withhold the ◇K, so that it can be used as a threat card later. Let us assume that West continues a diamond which you duck again and ruff in hand. Now are conditions right for a squeeze? You have all the remaining tricks but one: that's good. You have both a diamond and a club threat against one hand - East: that's good. Entries do not appear to be a problem.

Can you see the ending?

HAND 25 • *Now or Never*

Answer Part 2

This hand *can* be made, and the declarer at Table 2 found a way. He also ruffed the diamond continuation at trick two, but he didn't attack trumps right away. First, he cashed the three spade winners, then the ♣A, and the ♣K. At this critical juncture, he did not continue with the third high club but led the ♣4 instead! There is no effective counter to this extraordinary play.

If East continues now with a fourth round of clubs, declarer can ruff with the queen of trumps in dummy and lose only one more trick, the ace of trumps. Alternatively, if the defence continues with the ace and another trump, South can simply finish drawing trumps and claim, his tenth trick being the ♣Q. Either way, the defence makes only the ace of trumps, one club, and one diamond.

HAND 26 • *Marked Finesse*

Answer Part 2

This hand *can* be made. The solution is to win the opening spade lead in the closed hand and at trick two to lead the ♣Q! West wins with the king and continues with another spade. Dummy's ♠K wins this trick and you continue with the ♣10. It doesn't matter whether or not East covers with the jack, you will remain in dummy or return to it with a third club for the successful finesse against the ◇K.

HAND 27 • *Trump Control*

Answer Part 2

This hand *can* be made. After cashing the ♡A and ♡K in dummy, you can retain control of the hand by leading a diamond away from the ace. But not just any diamond will do: you must lead the ◇Q since you cannot afford to let East gain the lead to play clubs. West wins the ◇K and the best he can do is to continue diamonds. You ruff in hand and draw the outstanding trumps, discarding clubs from dummy.

You continue by leading a spade, and West must duck. A high spade wins in dummy and now you ruff another diamond with the last trump in your hand. You are now out of trumps but you still control the diamond suit. You now lead another spade. West wins but with the ◇A still in dummy he cannot cash any winners and must give dummy the lead. North will win the return and you can cash two spade winners and a diamond winner to make your contract with six trump tricks, three spades, and the ◇A.

HAND 28 • *Squeeze Possibilities*

Answer Part 2

This hand **cannot** be made, but West must be on his toes. Ducking the opening lead, South ruffs the second diamond and plans to execute a squeeze against East by reaching the following position:

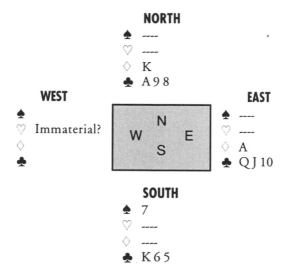

NORTH
♠ ----
♡ ----
◇ K
♣ A 9 8

WEST
♠
♡ Immaterial?
◇
♣

EAST
♠ ----
♡ ----
◇ A
♣ Q J 10

SOUTH
♠ 7
♡ ----
◇ ----
♣ K 6 5

On the last trump North discards a club and East is in trouble: he must discard a club in order to retain the ◇A. West must therefore grimly hang on to his three small clubs, taking the setting trick with the ♣7 at trick thirteen!

HAND 29 • *Have A Heart*

NORTH
♠ A Q 4
♡ J 9 7 6 3
◇ Q 9 5
♣ 5 2

WEST
♠ 7 6 3
♡ 10 8
◇ K 10 6 4
♣ K 10 7 6

EAST
♠ 2
♡ 5 4 2
◇ A J 8 7 3 2
♣ J 8 3

SOUTH
♠ K J 10 9 8 5
♡ A K Q
◇ ----
♣ A Q 9 4

Contract: 6♠
Opening Lead: ♠3

HAND 30 • *Elimination Exercise*

NORTH
♠ A K
♡ K
◇ J 8 4 2
♣ J 7 6 5 4 3

WEST
♠ Q J 7 4 2
♡ Q 9 8 5
◇ K 10
♣ K Q

EAST
♠ 10 9 8 6 5 3
♡ 7 6 3 2
◇ 9 6 3
♣ ----

SOUTH
♠ ----
♡ A J 10 4
◇ A Q 7 5
♣ A 10 9 8 2

Contract: 6♣
Opening Lead: ♣K

HAND 31 • *See-Saw*

NORTH
♠ 7
♡ 8 4
♢ K Q J 9 8 6 2
♣ A 7 6

WEST
♠ 4 2
♡ Q J 7 3 2
♢ 5 4
♣ K 10 9 3

```
        N
    W       E
        S
```

EAST
♠ K Q 10 8 5 3
♡ K 9 6
♢ A 10
♣ 5 4

SOUTH
♠ A J 9 6
♡ A 10 5
♢ 7 3
♣ Q J 8 2

Contract: 3NT
Opening Lead: ♡3

HAND 32 • *Small Magic*

NORTH
♠ J 4 3 2
♡ 9 8 2
♢ 9 3 2
♣ Q 8 5

WEST
♠ 10 9 8
♡ K J 6
♢ J 6 5 4
♣ J 7 3

```
        N
    W       E
        S
```

EAST
♠ 7 6 5
♡ 10 7 4 3
♢ Q 8 7
♣ K 9 4

SOUTH
♠ A K Q
♡ A Q 5
♢ A K 10
♣ A 10 6 2

Contract: 3NT
Opening Lead: ♠10

HAND 29 • *Have A Heart*

Answer Part 1

If we count winners, this hand looks pretty easy. You have six spade winners, five hearts, and a club for twelve. So what's the problem? If you count losers, you note that you have three potential club losers. You plan to throw two clubs on dummy's good hearts, but unfortunately the heart suit is blocked. You must dispose of the high hearts in your hand before the suit can be run in dummy and this must be done before drawing all the trumps since dummy's only entries are in the trump suit.

You can try cashing the top hearts after drawing only two rounds of trumps, but then West ruffs in on the third heart. Now there are only two hearts left to dispose of club losers in your hand and ultimately you will have to lose a club as well.

Can you find your way around the heart blockage?

HAND 30 • *Elimination Exercise*

Answer Part 1

It appears that there are two losers on this hand, a club and a diamond, since the $\diamond$K is offside. Two spade discards from South's hand are no help and a heart pitch from the North hand is equally useless. There is a chance to set up an additional heart trick with a ruffing finesse, but this still does not provide enough discards to get rid of the diamond loser. The only chance therefore is an elimination and throw-in -- that is, you must remove all the exit cards from the West hand and then throw him in on a club.

But how do you perform the elimination? Clearly, you must win the ♣A. Suppose you now lead a heart to the king and cash the top spades, throwing diamonds. If you now throw West in, he appears to be endplayed, but it turns out that a heart return into your tenace is safe, since the third heart trick does you no good.

Can this hand be made?

HAND 31 • See-Saw

Answer Part 1

As declarer, the first thing you do is count winners: you have six diamonds after knocking out the ace, two clubs, a spade, and a heart. So you appear to have enough tricks. Therefore, one goal for the defence is to remove dummy's entry to the diamonds, and the obvious way to do this is to force out the ♣A by leading the king. Declarer does have a counter to this plan: he can duck the ♣K and win the ♣Q if clubs are continued.

Are there any more twists to this plot? Can this hand be made?

HAND 32 • Small Magic

Answer Part 1

This hand, along with several others in this book, was created by the late and great Hungarian bridge player, Robert Darvas. Making 3NT on this hand seems impossible, but is there a way? South has seven top tricks after the opening spade lead -- three spades, a heart, two diamonds, and a club. With the 3-3 break in clubs, that suit can provide an eighth trick eventually. If you could get to dummy to cash the ♠J that would help a lot. Cashing the top three spades seems like a good start, but can you see a route to dummy after that? Is there an endplay of some sort? What about the club suit?

Is there a line of attack for the defence while all this is going on? Can this hand be made?

HAND 29 • *Have A Heart*

Answer Part 2

This hand *can* be made. The solution is to win the opening lead on the board, lead a diamond, and discard a heart on this trick! This *winner-on-loser* play solves all the problems. You win any continuation and cash the two top hearts left in your hand. You then draw the remaining trumps ending in dummy and now you are placed in the right hand to cash the rest of the hearts. Since you discarded a heart early in the hand you now get three pitches instead of only two on the hearts and you can throw all your club losers away. In practice you traded a club loser for a diamond loser, unblocking the heart suit at the same time.

HAND 30 • *Elimination Exercise*

Answer Part 2

This hand *can* be made although, in real life, it is unlikely you would actually succeed. As a double dummy problem it is a different matter. Losing a trump trick is unavoidable but you may avoid losing a diamond trick if you throw West in at an appropriate moment after eliminating the heart suit. The key to this hand is to note that the ♣A and ♠K do not provide useful discards since you can use the hearts to provide two diamond discards from dummy. Since they might as well be small spades, you can treat them as such.

Therefore, win the opening lead with the ♣A and begin the elimination of the heart suit. You start by cashing the ♡K and then ruff that *little* spade. You now cash the ♡A throwing the first diamond from dummy and then lead the ♡J to take the ruffing finesse. Suppose West covers: ruff the heart and ruff the ♠A to get back to your hand. You now cash the ♡10 throwing a second diamond from dummy. Now the hearts and spades have been eliminated and you can finally execute the throw-in. A club is led and West must return either a diamond into your ace-queen or a spade giving you a ruff and discard. You would, of course, discard dummy's third diamond, removing your diamond loser.

HAND 31 • *See-Saw*

Answer Part 2

This hand ***cannot*** be made. South cannot afford to take the initial heart lead since the defence will be able to cash four heart tricks when in with the ◇A. East, therefore, continues a second heart and declarer has to duck again. Now the defence must make the key play of leading the ♣K. declarer must duck the club to retain an entry to dummy's diamonds. The defence now has three tricks in and the ◇A to come. West now switches again, this time to a spade, setting up a fifth trick. The defence will come to two hearts, a club, a spade, and a diamond, defeating the contract.

HAND 32 • *Small Magic*

Answer Part 2

This hand ***can*** be made, since you can force an entry to dummy to score the ♠J and also establish a second trick in the club suit. The key to the hand is to save the ♣A for the fourth round! After cashing the three top spades, you lead the ♣10 from hand: this card is covered by the jack, queen, and king. East returns a small diamond (returning a heart will not help), won by your ace. You continue your plan by leading the ♣6 and West has to cover again: this trick goes ♣6, ♣7, ♣8, and ♣9.

Observe that by this time, as if by magic, dummy's ♣5 has become high (apart from the ace in South's hand) and all that remains to be done, after winning West's diamond continuation in hand, is to enter dummy by leading the ♣2 to the ♣5. Then you cash the ♠J, return to hand with the ♡A and cash the thirteenth club, the ♣A, as the game-going trick.

HAND 33 • *Mighty Strange*

NORTH
♠ J 4
♡ A 7 6
♢ 10 8 3
♣ A Q J 7 6

WEST
♠ A 10 9 8 5 3
♡ 8 4 3
♢ 4 2
♣ 8 2

EAST
♠ K 7
♡ J 10 9 2
♢ J 9 7 6
♣ K 5 4

SOUTH
♠ Q 6 2
♡ K Q 5
♢ A K Q 5
♣ 10 9 3

Contract: 3NT
Opening Lead: ♠10

HAND 34 • *A Question of Trumps*

NORTH
♠ K Q 8 4 3
♡ J 9 5 2
♢ J 6 3
♣ Q

WEST
♠ ----
♡ 8 6 4
♢ A K Q 10
♣ J 10 8 6 3 2

EAST
♠ J 10 9 7 5
♡ 7 3
♢ 8 5 2
♣ K 9 4

SOUTH
♠ A 6 2
♡ A K Q 10
♢ 9 7 4
♣ A 7 5

Contract: 4♡
Opening Lead: ♢A

HAND 35 • *Promotion*

NORTH
♠ 5 4
♡ Q 6 5 4 2
♢ 10 9 3 2
♣ A 2

WEST
♠ K 10 3
♡ K 9 8 7
♢ K Q
♣ J 10 9 4

EAST
♠ ----
♡ A J 10
♢ A J 7 6 5 4
♣ 8 7 6 5

SOUTH
♠ A Q J 9 8 7 6 2
♡ 3
♢ 8
♣ K Q 3

Contract: 4♠
Opening Lead: ♢K

HAND 36 • *A Helpful East*

NORTH
♠ 7 5 4 2
♡ 9 5 2
♢ K 7 5
♣ 7 6 2

WEST
♠ J 9 8 6 3
♡ 10 4
♢ J 10 9 8
♣ J 4

EAST
♠ Q 10
♡ K J 8 6
♢ 6 4 3 2
♣ 10 8 3

SOUTH
♠ A K
♡ A Q 7 3
♢ A Q
♣ A K Q 9 5

Contract: 6♣
Opening Lead: ♢J

HAND 33 • *Mighty Strange*

Answer Part 1

Depending on how you look at this hand it can seem obvious that declarer will have an easy time or that the defence will prevail. Let us assume that as East you make the obvious play of hopping up on the ♠K and returning a second spade at trick two. It doesn't matter if your partner ducks or wins the spade, declarer will finesse a club into your king and unfortunately you will have no more spades to return.

Declarer can win whatever you return and will make his contract with lots of tricks to spare: four clubs, three diamonds, three hearts, and a spade. Can you see a better approach to the defence? Look what happens if you *duck* the spade at trick one. Declarer wins the ♠Q, but now when declarer finesses into the ♣K you return the ♠K, partner overtakes, and declarer will be defeated.

Have you found the perfect solution for the defence?

HAND 34 • *A Question of Trumps*

Answer Part 1

As declarer in 4♡, you count your losers: the South hand has five potential losers -- three diamonds and two clubs. Under normal circumstances you would expect to be able to set up the spade suit for one or two discards and ruff one club in dummy. On the actual hand the spades break 5-0, so this plan will not work. You must therefore obtain two club ruffs in the South hand, and this means that you must delay drawing all the trumps for a while. This does however present some problems given the unfortunate spade situation.

What should West do at trick two? Can the defence find some way to prevent the ruffs? Can this hand be made?

Hand 35 • *Promotion*

Answer Part 1

When as declarer you count your losers, this hand appears quite secure: you have a diamond loser, a heart loser, and a spade loser. There is, however, a threat to your security, which is that West, who holds all of the outstanding trumps, will be able to promote a second trump trick. West will start this process by continuing diamonds, and on obtaining the lead with the trump king, can lead a heart to his partner's ace. East will then lead a third diamond promoting a trump trick in West's hand.

One option that you have is to discard a heart on the ◇Q, but East can counter this by overtaking the ◇Q with the ace, threatening to lead a third diamond for his partner to ruff. Since you can't let East win the trick, you therefore can't throw a heart on this diamond.

Is there a counter to this counter?

Hand 36 • *A Helpful East*

Answer Part 1

With the 3-2 trump break, South has only three losers, the ♡Q, ♡7, and ♡3: his goal must be to find a way to reduce his losers to one. He can use the ◇K as an entry to dummy for the heart finesse, but this will reduce his diamond winners to two.

When this hand was played in a rubber bridge game some years ago, South won the opening lead of the ◇J with the ace in his hand and drew trumps in three rounds. Now, he overtook the ◇Q with the ◇K in dummy to take the heart finesse. It won! Quite pleased with his performance so far, South played the ♡A and a small heart. Alas, hearts failed to break 3-3, and East took the ♡K and ♡J for one down.

"Bad luck, partner, there is just no way to make this slam," said a gloomy North.

Was he right?

Hand 33 • *Mighty Strange*

Answer Part 2

This hand *can* be made by an extraordinary holdup play. We will assume that West has opened a weak two bid, marking him with length in spades. At trick one, when North and East play low, South should play low as well! After refusing the spade trick, declarer cannot be prevented from making an overtrick! The spade suit is now set up -- but it is hopelessly blocked: East can cash the ♠K but after that there is no entry to the West hand for the rest of the spade suit. Declarer finesses the club into the East hand and comes to three diamonds, four clubs, and three hearts. Declarer has no spade tricks at all but more than enough tricks for his contract.

Hand 34 • *A Question of Trumps*

Answer Part 2

This hand *cannot* be made, but the defence must be very careful. The goal of the defence is to prevent declarer from obtaining his two club ruffs in dummy and the key to doing this is to attack his communications. You must therefore first cash all three diamonds, in order to prevent declarer's throwing you in on a diamond in the endgame, giving him a safe way back to his hand. You must then lead a trump! Declarer plans to use the trump suit to get back to his hand after club ruffs, so therefore you must remove one of these trump entries before he can begin ruffing clubs.

Declarer wins the trump, plays the ♣A, and ruffs a club. He can return to his hand with a trump to ruff another club, but after this club ruff we arrive at the moment of truth. If you have cashed out the diamond suit dummy has only spades left and declarer is now forced to lead a spade which you will ruff, defeating the contract.

Hand 35 • *Promotion*

Answer Part 2

This hand *can* be made. After the ◇K holds, West continues with his second diamond, trying to promote two trump tricks for his partner, East overtakes with the ◇A, and as declarer you have to ruff. But you do have a counter to this defence. You cross to dummy with the ♣A and continue with a diamond. East has to cover and you ruff this trick with the ace of trumps, conceding a second trump trick to West. Now you cash the ♣K and ruff your last club in dummy. Then you play the last diamond, now high, and discard your losing heart. West scores two trump tricks, but you still make your contract.

Hand 36 • *A Helpful East*

Answer Part 2

A helpful East pointed out that this hand *can* be made with a superior line of play. After winning the first trick with the ◇A, South should draw no more than one round of trumps and then lead a low heart, giving up the inevitable heart loser early. He can win the diamond return in dummy and finesse the ♡Q. When it wins, South draws a second round of trumps and then cashes the ♡A. If hearts are 3-3 there is no harm to this play; however, if hearts are 4-2 the hand can only be made if the hand with the long trump has the long hearts. Luck is with declarer when he finds East with four hearts and also three trumps. He can now ruff the last heart in dummy, and cross back to hand with a spade to draw the last trump and claim his slam.

HAND 37 • *Good Play*

NORTH
- ♠ K 6
- ♡ 3
- ◇ Q 8 7 2
- ♣ A J 10 9 8 4

WEST
- ♠ 8 7 4 2
- ♡ Q 7 5
- ◇ A 4
- ♣ K 6 5 3

	N	
W		E
	S	

EAST
- ♠ A J 10 9 3
- ♡ K J 10 6 2
- ◇ 6
- ♣ Q 7

SOUTH
- ♠ Q 5
- ♡ A 9 8 4
- ◇ K J 10 9 5 3
- ♣ 2

Contract: 5◇
Opening Lead: ◇A

HAND 38 • *A Sure Thing*

NORTH
- ♠ K 8 5 4
- ♡ 7 3
- ◇ A K 7
- ♣ J 6 5 3

WEST
- ♠ A 6 2
- ♡ Q J 9 8 2
- ◇ Q 10 2
- ♣ K 9

	N	
W		E
	S	

EAST
- ♠ 3
- ♡ K 10
- ◇ J 9 6 5 4
- ♣ Q 10 8 7 4

SOUTH
- ♠ Q J 10 9 7
- ♡ A 6 5 4
- ◇ 8 3
- ♣ A 2

Contract: 4♠
Opening Lead: ♠A

HAND 39 • *One Chance Only*

NORTH
- ♠ J 10 6
- ♡ A Q J 8 5
- ◇ K 3
- ♣ K 5 2

WEST
- ♠ K 7 4
- ♡ 9 3
- ◇ J 10 9 7
- ♣ A Q 10 8

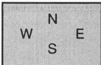

EAST
- ♠ 8 2
- ♡ K 6 4
- ◇ Q 6 5 4 2
- ♣ 9 6 3

SOUTH
- ♠ A Q 9 5 3
- ♡ 10 7 2
- ◇ A 8
- ♣ J 7 4

Contract: 4♠
Opening Lead: ◇J

HAND 40 • *Dangerous Hand*

NORTH
- ♠ 10 8 7 4 3
- ♡ J 10
- ◇ A 5 2
- ♣ A Q 5

WEST
- ♠ K Q 6
- ♡ 8 4 3
- ◇ Q 10 8 4
- ♣ J 7 4

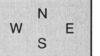

EAST
- ♠ J 5
- ♡ ----
- ◇ K J 9 7 6 3
- ♣ K 10 8 6 2

SOUTH
- ♠ A 9 2
- ♡ A K Q 9 7 6 5 2
- ◇ ----
- ♣ 9 3

Contract: 6♡
Opening Lead: ◇4

Hand 37 • *Good Play*

Answer Part 1

West starts off with the best defence: ace and another trump. If trumps are not led early, South can crossruff for the first few tricks, ruffing all his heart losers in dummy and returning to hand with club ruffs; after that he will give up the ♠A and will score five diamond tricks in hand, a spade, a heart, and three heart ruffs in dummy for eleven tricks. On trump leads, however, you can only obtain two heart ruffs in dummy so your only chance as declarer is to set up the club suit. The problem is that you do not have enough entries to dummy to establish the club suit and get there to cash clubs. Since you must ruff three clubs to set up the suit, you require four entries. You have a club entry, the ♣A, and two entries on heart ruffs. The ♠K might have been an entry but unfortunately East holds the ace. Can you find a way to produce another entry to dummy? Can the defence prevent it?

Hand 38 • *A Sure Thing*

Answer Part 1

Again West starts things off with the best defence, ace and another trump. Now analyze your chances: you have a spade loser, a club loser, and up to three heart losers. You can always ruff at least one heart in dummy, leaving four losers, so your goal is to try to ruff a second heart: to do this you want to lose a heart trick to East. Say you win the second trump in dummy and lead a heart: if East rises with the king you duck, and if East plays low you win the ace and lead another heart. East gains the lead and has no trump to return, so you can now get two ruffs in dummy to make your contract.

Do you see any problems with this plan? Is there a better line?

Hand 39 • *One Chance Only*

Answer Part 1

Declarer wins the opening diamond lead in dummy and takes the spade finesse. At this point declarer has four potential losers: a spade, a heart, and two clubs. With the heart finesse off, declarer must set up hearts and then discard club losers on the established hearts. The defence must find a way to take two club tricks before declarer can run hearts. West can switch to a club when he is in on the ♡K, but which club should West lead? Obviously a small club will not work because declarer can duck it to the jack.

What about a different continuation? Who will win this race?

Hand 40 • *Dangerous Hand*

Answer Part 1

Once again, you find yourself in a six-level contract with eleven tricks: eight hearts, a spade, a diamond, and a club. If necessary the twelfth trick could come from the club finesse (which won't work on this particular lie of the cards). Another alternative is to set up the spade suit for the twelfth trick. The idea is to discard a spade on the ♢A and then play ace and another spade. Then you enter dummy with a trump and ruff a spade. You draw trumps ending in dummy, and cash a spade for the twelfth trick.

However, with the bad trump break West can foil this plan by winning the second spade and leading a club, prematurely removing your dummy entry. What now?

Hand 37 • *Good Play*

Answer Part 2

This hand *can* be made by establishing the clubs. After winning the second trump you begin by playing the ♣A and ruffing a club, noting the fall of the ♣Q. Now you make the key play: you lead the ♠Q, and you don't care who has the ♠A or even whether he wins or ducks. If the ♠A takes this trick you now have an extra entry to dummy to set up and run clubs.

However, let us say that East ducks the ♠Q. Now you can establish clubs with one fewer entry by conceding a club to the ♣K, the only remaining high club in enemy hands, and discarding your last spade from hand. This loser-on-loser play allows you to set up the clubs while there is a still a trump left in dummy to get back there to run the established clubs. The only tricks lost are a diamond and a club.

Hand 38 • *A Sure Thing*

Answer Part 2

This hand *cannot* be made. West initiates the best defence by leading the ace and another trump. South can improve his chances by winning the second trick in dummy and leading a heart from there: if East goes up with the king, South ducks. But the defence has the last laugh: a sure way to defeat the contract is for East to throw away his ♡K at trick two, on the second trump lead. Now declarer cannot duck a heart to East's hand; West can win any heart that declarer ducks with the ♡J and will be in to lead a third trump, limiting declarer to one heart ruff in dummy.

Hand 39 • _One Chance Only_

Answer Part 2

This hand *cannot* be made. After declarer takes the spade finesse, West must immediately switch to a club to establish
the defensive club tricks. Neither a small club nor the ♣A
works, but there is a winning play: you must lead the ♣Q.
Declarer will win the ♣K, draw the remaining trumps, and
then try the heart finesse. But when East is in on the ♡K, he
can lead a club through declarer's jack to your ♣A10. Nor
will it help South to play hearts first: East will duck the first
heart, and, if declarer ducks a second heart before drawing
trump, East can give West a ruff with his third heart and the
defence will take a spade, a heart, a club, and a heart ruff. If
declarer switches back to trumps after the first heart is
ducked, the defence plays clubs as before. South can surely
complain of bad luck: two losing finesses and, worst of all,
excellent play by his opponents.

HAND 40 • _Dangerous Hand_

Answer Part 2

This hand *can* be made but it requires some ingenuity.
Declarer must cover the opening lead of the ♢4 with the ♢5
and discard a spade on the trick. "Must cover", you say? Yes,
because otherwise a clever East could play the ♢3, allowing
West to hold the lead. West would now switch to clubs, removing a crucial entry to the North hand. The key to this
hand is to prevent the danger hand, West, from gaining the
lead.

On winning the first trick, suppose East continues with
a spade (best): you win the ♠A, play a trump to dummy's ten,
discard the ♠9 on the ♢A and ruff a spade. Now you lead
another small trump to the jack and ruff one more spade, establishing the suit. After drawing the outstanding trump,
you can cross to the ♣A and discard your club loser on the
♠10.

SECTION 3

REALLY
CHALLENGING

HAND 41 • *Go Latin*

NORTH
♠ 3
♡ A K 7
◇ K J 10 6 5
♣ K J 8 6

WEST
♠ A 9 2
♡ J 10 6 5 4
◇ A 7 2
♣ 10 2

EAST
♠ Q 5
♡ 9 8 3 2
◇ 9 8 3
♣ A 9 7 4

SOUTH
♠ K J 10 8 7 6 4
♡ Q
◇ Q 4
♣ Q 5 3

Contract: 4♠
Opening Lead: ♣10

HAND 42 • *Oriental Wisdom*

NORTH
♠ A 8 3
♡ 9 7 5
◇ K 5 3
♣ Q J 10 9

WEST
♠ K Q 10 9 7 2
♡ A Q J 6 2
◇ J 2
♣ ----

EAST
♠ J 6 4
♡ 10 4
◇ 8
♣ K 8 7 6 5 3 2

SOUTH
♠ 5
♡ K 8 3
◇ A Q 10 9 7 6 4
♣ A 4

Contract: 5◇
Opening Lead: ♠K

HAND 43 • *Best Friend*

NORTH
♠ J 4
♡ 6 3
◇ K 8 4 3
♣ A K 9 4 2

WEST
♠ A Q 3
♡ Q 8 4
◇ Q 9 6 2
♣ 8 7 3

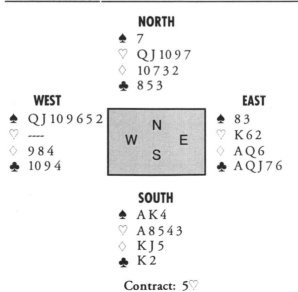

EAST
♠ 7 6
♡ K J 10 9 5 2
◇ J 5
♣ Q J 10

SOUTH
♠ K 10 9 8 5 2
♡ A 7
◇ A 10 7
♣ 6 5

Contract: 4♠
Opening Lead: ♡Q

HAND 44 • *Par Contest*

NORTH
♠ 7
♡ Q J 10 9 7
◇ 10 7 3 2
♣ 8 5 3

WEST
♠ Q J 10 9 6 5 2
♡ ----
◇ 9 8 4
♣ 10 9 4

EAST
♠ 8 3
♡ K 6 2
◇ A Q 6
♣ A Q J 7 6

SOUTH
♠ A K 4
♡ A 8 5 4 3
◇ K J 5
♣ K 2

Contract: 5♡
Opening Lead: ♠Q

HAND 41 • *Go Latin*

Answer Part 1

West starts the ♣10, North covers with the jack in dummy, and East ducks, hoping to give his partner a club ruff when West is in on the ♠A. If we ignore ruffs, South is in pretty good shape. With the favourable situation in the spade suit, there are only three losers off the top (a diamond, a club, and a spade), so declarer's problem is to prevent the club ruff. The only hope appears to be discards on the heart suit.

Suppose declarer starts with the ♡A and ♡K, throwing his second club. When West is in with the ♠A, he can still return a club to his partner's ace, and now a third club promotes a trump trick for the defence (if South ruffs low West will overruff, while if he ruffs with the ♠10, West will eventually score the ♠9).

Can you see a different strategy for declarer? Is there a counter for the defence?

HAND 42 • *Oriental Wisdom*

Answer Part 1

This hand appears to be a Chinese puzzle. You must set up clubs in order to discard your heart losers, and you must do this without letting East in to lead a heart through your king. You also have to draw trumps before playing clubs, since West can ruff the first round, and the defence will ultimately score at least two heart tricks.

Therefore you draw two rounds of trumps, ending in dummy with the ◇K, you take the club finesse and cash the ♣A. You can then return to dummy once with the ◇5, assuming you saved your ◇3. Now you can force out the ♣K by leading the queen and ruffing when East covers, but you cannot get back to dummy to enjoy the established club.

You read once about a similar hand where ducking the opening spade lead was right, but how would that help here? Assuming West continues a spade, you can throw a club away and draw two rounds of trumps ending in dummy. But the stupid ♣A is in your way.

Can this hand be made?

HAND 43 • *Best Friend*

Answer Part 1

At first blush, it appears that declarer has four losers, a heart, two spades and a diamond. However, with the 3-3 club break, you can establish clubs to provide a discard for the third diamond. You must, of course, preserve your ◇K as an entry to dummy to cash the established clubs. However, if the defence attacks diamonds to destroy your communications, they may, in fact, lose their diamond winner along the way. This hand is clearly going to be a battle of timing and spot cards.

Can you see who the winner will be, declarer or the defence?

HAND 44 • *Par Contest*

Answer Part 1

This hand was actually constructed by the late Geoffrey Mott-Smith for the 1938 Bridge Olympics, a competition in which the players had to make "par" scores by correct bidding and play. North-South have sacrificed against their opponents' 4♠ contract. As declarer you see that you have no spade losers, a potential heart loser, two potential diamond losers, and two potential club losers, but with the favourable lie of the cards perhaps you can restrict your losers to one club and one diamond.

The obvious way to begin is to win the first spade, ruff a spade, and lead the ♡Q. West will cover the first or second heart, and you can now cross to dummy and lead a diamond. Should West duck or rise? Can you get back to the dummy enough times to make all the needed plays from the dummy? Leading the ◇10 will help, but....

The obvious question on this hand is: what is par -- making or defeating 5♡?

HAND 41 • *Go Latin*

Answer Part 2

This hand, which occurred in a recent South American championship, **cannot** be made against inspired defence. The opening lead was covered with the jack in dummy and ducked by East. Seeing the danger, declarer played ♡A, ♡K, and a third heart, discarding all the clubs from his hand and disrupting the communications between the defenders. If East returns a club now, West still has a club left. South can ruff low, cross to dummy on a diamond, and take the trump finesse; West will not be able to get to his partner's hand for the trump promotion.

But the defence found an effective counter. When East was in with the third heart he played a fourth heart, giving declarer a useless ruff-sluff. Declarer had to ruff in his hand and tried to enter dummy with a diamond, but West took his ◇A and played a fifth heart, which East ruffed with the queen. This play ensured two trump tricks for West and the contract was defeated.

HAND 42 • *Oriental Wisdom*

Answer Part 2

This hand *can* be made; in fact, it was played and made several years ago by the Taiwan expert Chien Hwa Wang. On the first trick he played the ♠3 from dummy and the ♠5 from his hand! When West continued with the ♠Q, Wang followed low again and ruffed in his hand with the ◇6. Next he cashed the ◇A and entered dummy by playing the ◇7 to the ◇K. A successful club finesse followed when East refused to cover the queen.

Wang now led the ♠A and discarded his ♣A on it! He continued with the ♣J and when East covered with the king, South ruffed with the ◇9. He returned to dummy by playing his carefully preserved ◇4 to the ◇5, then discarded two of his losing hearts on the ♣9 and ♣10. The only tricks Wang lost were a spade and a heart.

HAND 43 • _Best Friend_

Answer Part 2

This hand **cannot** be made, as was demonstrated by the British star, the late Rixi Markus. Playing with Italy's Benito Garozzo, who was West, Mrs. Markus overtook the opening lead with the ♡K, South winning the ♡A. Declarer entered dummy with a club and passed the ♠J, and Garozzo led another heart to his partner's nine.

Now, to prevent declarer's establishing the club suit, it was important to attack dummy's only entry, the ◇K. There was only one good way to do this and Mrs. Markus found it: she shifted to the ◇5! South had to win this in hand with the ace and he drove out the ♠A, but Garozzo returned a diamond to dummy's king, leaving South with an unavoidable diamond loser. Notice that the return of the ◇J at the trick five does not work, as West cannot continue the suit later without permitting the ◇10 to score in the closed hand.

HAND 44 • _Par Contest_

Answer Part 2

This hand **cannot** be made but it takes extraordinary technique to defeat 5♡. South wins the ♠A, ruffs a spade, and then leads the ♡Q from dummy. To defeat the hand, you as East must duck the ♡Q and cover the ♡J. South will then cross to the dummy with a third round of trumps and lead the ◇10. Now comes the key play.

If you duck the ◇10, South just continues with another diamond, guaranteeing a second diamond trick whether you take your ace at this point or not. South has the choice of establishing the thirteenth diamond as the game-going trick or crossing to dummy by ruffing the ♠K with dummy's last trump and leading a club up to the king.

Suppose instead that you rise with the ◇A on the ◇10: you are now endplayed -- whether you lead diamonds or clubs, you will give South an opportunity to finesse and South will still have one more entry to dummy for his last finesse.

Do you see the winning play? You must cover the ◇10 with the queen! Now South does not have enough entries to lead up to both the ◇J and the ♣K! He cannot avoid losing three tricks in the minor suits.

HAND 45 • *Good Plan*

NORTH
♠ Q6532
♡ 843
◇ A32
♣ AK

WEST
♠ J109
♡ K102
◇ 75
♣ 97432

```
      N
  W       E
      S
```

EAST
♠ K874
♡ Q976
◇ 986
♣ 85

SOUTH
♠ A
♡ AJ5
◇ KQJ104
♣ QJ106

Contract: 6◇
Opening Lead: ♠J

HAND 46 • *You Have To See It*

NORTH
♠ KJ
♡ 1042
◇ 108
♣ KQJ1098

WEST
♠ Q84
♡ QJ97
◇ J763
♣ A3

```
      N
  W       E
      S
```

EAST
♠ 976532
♡ ----
◇ 52
♣ 76542

SOUTH
♠ A10
♡ AK8653
◇ AKQ94
♣ ----

Contract: 6NT
Opening Lead: ♡Q

Hand 47 • *Atrocious Luck*

NORTH
♠ 9 5 4 3
♡ Q 10 6 3 2
◇ A Q 6 3
♣ ----

WEST
♠ ----
♡ J 9 8 7 5 4
◇ K 9 5
♣ 9 8 5 4

EAST
♠ K Q J 10 8
♡ A K
◇ J 10 8 4
♣ Q 7

SOUTH
♠ A 7 6 2
♡ ----
◇ 7 2
♣ A K J 10 6 3 2

Contract: 6♣
Opening Lead: ♡7

HAND 48 • *Inspiration*

NORTH
♠ 8 3
♡ 7 6 2
◇ K J 6
♣ A Q J 8 6

WEST
♠ 7
♡ K Q J 9 4
◇ 10 7 2
♣ 7 5 4 3

EAST
♠ A K 4
♡ 10 8 5 3
◇ A Q 9 5
♣ K 2

SOUTH
♠ Q J 10 9 6 5 2
♡ A
◇ 8 4 3
♣ 10 9

Contract: 3♠
Opening Lead: ♡K

HAND 45 • _Good Plan_

Answer Part 1

After winning the opening lead perforce with the ♠A, you count your losers and note that you have two heart losers unless the ♡K and ♡Q are both onside. Unfortunately, that is not the case on this hand, so you must find a place to dispose of your second heart loser. No squeeze is possible since West can guard hearts and East can guard spades. The only alternative appears to be the establishment of the spade suit; however, with the ♠K guarded three times, there are two problems: lack of entries and lack of trumps. You will have to ruff three spades, but after drawing trumps you will only have two diamonds left.

Chances appear dim. Can this hand be made?

Hand 46 • _You Have To See It_

Answer Part 1

After winning the opening lead with the ♡K you take stock and realize that you have only seven tricks: two spades, two hearts, and three diamonds. If you give up a heart trick, West will be able to cash the ♣A. The only hope seems to be the club suit -- but it seems impossible to set up clubs and then find an entry to dummy to cash them, without giving up the lead in a red suit -- for down one!

There must be some trick here - can you see it? And is there any counter for the defence?

HAND 47 • *Atrocious Luck*

Answer Part 1

This hand occurred many years ago at a tournament in Holland. By some misunderstanding, the "impossible" contract of 6♣ was reached. Now that you're in it, can you make it?

After ruffing the opening lead, you cash the top two trumps and get the good news when the queen drops. As you can see, the diamond finesse also works so things are going well so far. At this point you have reached the grand total of ten tricks: seven clubs, two diamonds, and a spade. You can gain an eleventh trick by establishing a heart winner, but how can you find another trick (hint: a squeeze is involved)?

Can you find an ending that will let you make the hand? Can the defence counter?

HAND 48 • *Inspiration*

Answer Part 1

After winning the first trick with the ♡A as declarer, you find that you have a lot of losers: two spades and a diamond off the top, and possibly a club and two more diamonds depending on the lie of the cards. However, after drawing trumps you could play to set up the club suit. Since East will be on lead at that point, he will be unable to cash more than one diamond trick and your other diamond losers can go on the established club winners. East can make life difficult by ducking the first round of clubs (single dummy), but if you guess what he has done you are home. To begin executing your plan you start off by leading the ♣Q.

Will this plan work? Can the defence do anything?

HAND 45 • *Good Plan*

Answer Part 2

This difficult slam *can* be made by a somewhat unorthodox play. You win the first trick with the ♠A, play the king and ace of trumps, and ruff a spade. Returning to the dummy with a club, you ruff another spade. You need both remaining trumps, the one in your hand to ruff the penultimate spade and the one in dummy to provide an entry to cash the final spade. You continue by leading another club to the ace and ruffing out East's ♠K with the last trump in your hand.

When you now lead the ♣Q and discard a heart from the board, East is in trouble. If he ruffs in on this trick, you could win the heart return in hand and cash the ♣J discarding the last heart from dummy. At this point, dummy is high. Ducking the ♣Q does not help the defence either -- you continue with the ♣J and discard another heart from dummy. If East ducks again, you cash the ♡A and ruff a heart in dummy. That's twelve tricks and your slam.

HAND 46 • *You Have To See It*

Answer Part 2

This hand *can* be made but it is unlikely that you would do so in real life. You have to win the opening lead in your hand, lead the ♠10 and, if West follows low, finesse the ♠J in the dummy. Now you lead the ♣K and discard your ♠A on it: West is endplayed at trick four and must give you the dummy. A small spade, heart, or diamond allow you to reach dummy immediately, while if West returns a red jack you win in hand and can enter dummy with the ten in that suit. With access to dummy's clubs you wind up with twelve tricks: two spades, five clubs, two hearts and three diamonds.

HAND 47 • *Atrocious Luck*

Answer Part 2

This hand *can* be made; the declarer ruffed the opening heart lead, and cashed the two top clubs, catching East's queen. Next he led a diamond to the queen and ruffed a heart, East's ace falling. Here's how you proceed from here.

The plan is to set up a spade-diamond squeeze against East, and to do this you must remove the third diamond from West. You cash the ♣J, lead a diamond to the ace, and ruff a diamond, leaving East in control of that suit. Unfortunately, this also removes your entry to dummy to cash the diamond if East unguards it. You solve this problem in an extraordinary way. You ruff the third diamond with the ♣10, establishing West's ♣9, and now give West his club trick. But he is endplayed, having only hearts left. West must lead a heart into dummy's tenace, giving you the trick back and putting you back in dummy.

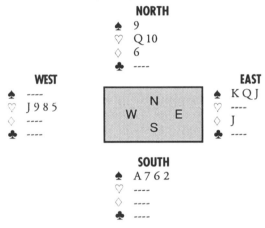

NORTH
♠ 9
♡ Q 10
♢ 6
♣ ----

WEST
♠ ----
♡ J 9 8 5
♢ ----
♣ ----

EAST
♠ K Q J
♡ ----
♢ J
♣ ----

SOUTH
♠ A 7 6 2
♡ ----
♢ ----
♣ ----

Dummy wins the ♡10, East and South discarding spades. When you now lead the ♡Q, East has to resign. It requires great luck and extraordinarily good play to make this slam.

HAND 48 • *Inspiration*

Answer Part 2

This hand *cannot* be made if East finds an inspired play. After winning the opening lead with the ♡A, declarer starts leads the ♠Q. East wins with the ♠K and returns a club, in order to knock out the entry to the club suit before East's last trump is drawn. The defensive plan is to sacrifice one trick, the ♣K, for two tricks in diamonds. Of course, it requires a very specific distribution for South if this play to be right .

After your club switch, when declarer plays a second spade, you rise with the ace and play a second club. Declarer makes two club tricks but cannot cash any other clubs, since you can ruff the third round and declarer will inevitably lose three diamond tricks to go one down.

HAND 49 • *Take Transfer*

NORTH
♠ K 9 5
♡ A 5 3 2
◇ 8 4 2
♣ A K 10

WEST
♠ 2
♡ K 7 6 4
◇ J 10 9 7
♣ 9 8 7 3

```
      N
   W     E
      S
```

EAST
♠ J 4 3
♡ J 9 8
◇ A K Q
♣ Q J 6 4

SOUTH
♠ A Q 10 8 7 6
♡ Q 10
◇ 6 5 3
♣ 5 2

Contract: 4♠
Opening Lead: ◇J

HAND 50 • *Searching for Trick 12*

NORTH
♠ A K 10 8 6 4
♡ 6 3
◇ K 4 3
♣ Q J

WEST
♠ J
♡ 9 7 5
◇ Q J 9 7 6
♣ 10 8 5 3

```
      N
   W     E
      S
```

EAST
♠ Q 9 7 5 2
♡ Q J 10 4
◇ 10 8
♣ 9 4

SOUTH
♠ 3
♡ A K 8 2
◇ A 5 2
♣ A K 7 6 2

Contract: 6♣
Opening Lead: ♠J

HAND 51 • *Cryptic Line*

NORTH
♠ J 5
♡ 8 7 4
♢ 10 8 5 4
♣ 9 7 3 2

WEST
♠ 7 4 2
♡ Q 5 2
♢ K Q J 6 3
♣ A 10

EAST
♠ 8 6 3
♡ 10 3
♢ A 9 7 2
♣ K Q 6 5

SOUTH
♠ A K Q 10 9
♡ A K J 9 6
♢ ----
♣ J 8 4

Contract: 4♡
Opening Lead: ♢K

HAND 52 • *Control Yourself*

NORTH
♠ K Q J
♡ A J 8
♢ A 9 6
♣ K Q J 10

WEST
♠ 10 9 8 2
♡ 5 3
♢ K J 4 3 2
♣ 8 5

EAST
♠ 6
♡ K Q 9 7 2
♢ Q 10 8 5
♣ A 4 3

SOUTH
♠ A 7 5 4 3
♡ 10 6 4
♢ 7
♣ 9 7 6 2

Contract: 4♠
Opening Lead: ♣8

HAND 49 • *Take Transfer*

Answer Part 1

The defence starts with a top diamond. Since he cannot effectively tackle hearts or clubs, East continues with the ◇K and ◇Q and exits with a trump. You, as declarer, win in your hand and take stock.

There are two obvious ways to play this hand, single dummy. One is a double club finesse, which wins if West has both the ♣Q and ♣J. The other way is a squeeze, which wins if either defender has both the ♣Q and ♣J (or any six clubs) and the ♡K. To operate the squeeze, you begin by cashing the ♡A and then run all the spades. If all the high cards are held by one defender, that player will either have to unguard the clubs or throw away the ♡K. However, as we can see, neither of these lines work.

Can the hand be made? And, by the way, is cashing the high diamonds early in the hand the correct defence?

HAND 50 • *Searching for Trick 12*

Answer Part 1

You don't have to think too long before playing from the dummy on this hand. You must win the opening lead with the ♠A, since if you don't, East's spade continuation at trick two will defeat you via a trump promotion.

You have eleven tricks: five clubs, two diamonds, two hearts, and two spades. It does not appear possible to set up a spade trick given the poor split, while ruffing a heart creates a trump loser, so the best chance seems to be some kind of squeeze. The problem is that you cannot duck a trick to rectify the count without drawing trumps. However, there might be some sort of strip and endplay on East by squeezing him out of his idle cards and forcing him to lead a spade into the dummy from his minor tenace.

Can you find trick twelve?

HAND 51 • *Cryptic Line*

Answer Part 1

After ruffing the diamond lead South has four potential losers -- a trump and three clubs. South plays two high trumps before leading spades, planning to shed dummy's clubs. Since West cannot ruff in until the fourth round of spades, South has time to discard two of dummy's clubs, one on the third spade and one on the fourth spade as West ruffs. Now he concedes a club, and ruffs one in dummy for trick ten.

However, there is a flaw in this plan: West can refuse to trump the fourth or fifth spade! South is now suddenly at the end of his rope. When he leads a club from his hand, West goes up with the ♣A and cashes the ♡Q. East still has two club winners, and holds declarer to nine tricks.

Can you see an alternative line of play?

HAND 52 • *Control Yourself*

Answer Part 1

At first this hand looks deceptively simple: it appears that you have five spades, three clubs, and two aces for ten tricks. Unfortunately, there is a problem once the trumps break 4-1.

East ducks the opening club lead, intending to give his partner a club ruff when the defence regains the lead. After winning the first trick, you can draw three rounds of trumps, but the problem now is to get back to your hand to draw the last trump without losing control. If you continue clubs now, East can win and give his partner a club ruff with his fourth trump, so that tactic won't work. If you ruff a diamond back to hand and draw the last trump, you will lose control of the hand: you still have to give up the ♣A and you have no trumps left to stop the diamond onslaught.

Is there any solution to these problems?

HAND 49 • _Take Transfer_

Answer Part 2

On the lie of the cards, this hand **cannot** be made. At first it appears that you can execute a squeeze by transferring the guard from one defender to another. You lead the ♡Q, West must cover with the ♡K, and East is left guarding both clubs and hearts. You do this early while you still have a trump re-entry to your hand to run the trump suit. You now run all the trumps, arriving at this ending:

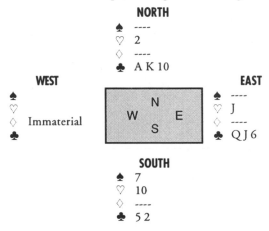

NORTH
♠ ----
♡ 2
♢ ----
♣ A K 10

WEST
♠
♡
♢ Immaterial
♣

EAST
♠ ----
♡ J
♢ ----
♣ Q J 6

SOUTH
♠ 7
♡ 10
♢ ----
♣ 5 2

East is squeezed on the last trump and you must make the last three tricks.

But what if the defence does not cash diamonds early? Suppose East switches to a trump at trick two? You win and lead a diamond; East leads another trump. You win and lead a diamond; East leads a third trump. Now you cannot transfer the heart menace to East and still get back to your hand to run spades. And East cannot be endplayed: if you draw trumps and throw East in, he cashes whatever diamond winners remain in his hand and exits safely with the ♣Q.

HAND 50 • _Searching for Trick 12_

Answer Part 2

This hand **cannot** be made but it requires very careful play by the defence. A number of squeezes are possible, but the problem is always entries. For example, suppose you cash the club honours in dummy and cross to your hand on the ♢A to draw trumps. If you now duck a heart to set up a double squeeze or a major suit squeeze, the defence can return a heart destroying your communications. You will need to cash the ◇K to remove an idle card from East's hand and there is then no way to get between the two hands.

The best chance is a strip and endplay on East, if he is not alert. After cashing dummy's club honours, you lead a heart from dummy. East must split his honours to preserve the ♡4 which will be a very useful card later. You then play all three of your remaining clubs. This is the position:

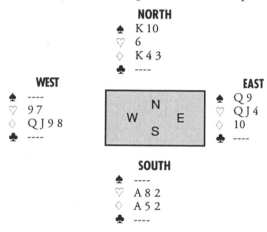

NORTH
♠ K 10
♡ 6
◇ K 4 3
♣ ----

WEST
♠ ----
♡ 9 7
◇ Q J 9 8
♣ ----

EAST
♠ Q 9
♡ Q J 4
◇ 10
♣ ----

SOUTH
♠ ----
♡ A 8 2
◇ A 5 2
♣ ----

South now cashes the ◇A and ◇K, intending to throw East in with a heart honour for a spade endplay. However, if East discards the ♡J on the second diamond, declarer is doomed. If he tries to play ace and another heart, East throws his second heart honour under the ace, ensuring that West (who has diamond winners) will take the defence's heart trick.

HAND 51 • *Cryptic Line*

Answer Part 2

This hand *can* be made. Ruffing the opening lead, South has to cash the ♡A and ♡K, then go to the board with the ♠J and ruff another diamond, leaving himself with only one trump. He now continues as before with top spades, West discarding a diamond as before (it would not help him to ruff). South discards two clubs from dummy and leads his last spade. Again, West cannot profitably ruff, so he discards another diamond, whereupon declarer ruffs his spade winner with dummy's last trump and plays still another diamond which he ruffs with the last trump in his own hand. This way South scores the first ten tricks (six hearts and four spades) to make his contact.

HAND 52 • *Control Yourself*

Answer Part 2

This hand *can* be made but you must be prepared to give up trump control. You are willing to concede a trump trick to West, because you plan to endplay the defence, losing only one heart trick.

East ducks the opening lead, so you begin by playing the ◇A at trick two and ruffing a diamond. You cross back to dummy on a trump and ruff a second diamond, and now you play a second club. East wins and plays a third club (red suits are worse). If West ruffs and returns a heart, you duck, and East, who has only red cards, is endplayed. If he returns a diamond you ruff in hand with the ♠A, and dummy is high after you draw trumps with the ♠QJ.

West can refuse to ruff the club, pitching a heart instead. This is the ending:

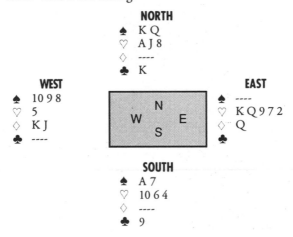

```
                    NORTH
                 ♠  K Q
                 ♡  A J 8
                 ◇  ----
                 ♣  K
      WEST                      EAST
   ♠  10 9 8                 ♠  ----
   ♡  5                      ♡  K Q 9 7 2
   ◇  K J                    ◇  Q
   ♣  ----                   ♣
                    SOUTH
                 ♠  A 7
                 ♡  10 6 4
                 ◇  ----
                 ♣  9
```

You lead the ♡J, and East wins to find himself once again endplayed! If he leads a heart, West can ruff, but that is the last trick for the defence, while if East returns a diamond you ruff in hand. This is your seventh trick, and you have two high trumps in dummy to come. West cannot prevent your making a tenth trick. If he ruffs one of your winners and leads a trump you can claim, and if he leads a diamond you can make your three trumps separately.